D1271515

ALSO BY DAVID COOPER

*Dialectics of Liberation*
(editor)

*Psychiatry and Anti-Psychiatry*

*Reason and Violence*
(with R. D. Laing)

# THE DEATH OF THE FAMILY

# THE DEATH

PANTHEON BOOKS

# OF THE FAMILY

by DAVID COOPER

A DIVISION OF RANDOM HOUSE, NEW YORK

 Published in the United States by Pantheon Books, a division of Random House, Inc., New York.

Library of Congress Catalog Card Number: 72-118019

ISBN: 0-394-42156-6

Manufactured in the United States of America
by Haddon Craftsmen, Inc., Scranton, Pa.

9 8 7 6 5 4 3 2

I THINK that dedications are important personal statements, not merely formal acts. Therefore I will not dedicate this book to Ronald Laing, to whom I owe more than any other man on earth, or under it, or to Juliet Mitchell, with whom I lived and loved during the writing of it. They know my feelings anyhow.

During the end of the writing of this book, which in fact is more a provocation than a book against the family, I went through a profound spiritual and bodily crisis that amounted to the death-and-rebirth experience of renewal that I speak of in these pages. The people who sat with me and tended to me with immense kindliness and concern during the worst of this crisis were my brother Peter and sister-in-law Carol and their small daughters. Just as a true family should. I taught Heidi, aged four, the language of water and how to shake hands with the branch of an oak and say hello and then listen to the astonishingly different answers that trees give. What she taught me runs far deeper.

I have made no attempt to simplify some of the ambiguities and paradoxes in this book, since it is for those who have ears and can hear, but above all for those who can hear and then listen and then act.

# CONTENTS

# THE DEATH OF THE FAMILY

# On Being Born into a Family

IN THIS CRITIQUE of the family most of my paradigmatic references will concern primarily the nuclear family unit in capitalist society in this part of this century. The broader reference, however, and most of my general statements will cover the social functioning of the family as an ideological conditioning device (the nonhuman phrasing is deliberate and necessary) in any exploitative society—slave society, feudal society, capitalist society from its most primitive phase in the last century to the neo-colonizing societies in the first world today. It also applies to the first-world working class, second-world societies and third-world countries, insofar as these have been indoctrinated into a spurious consciousness that, as we shall see, is definitive of the secret suicide pact conducted by the bourgeois family unit, the unit that labels itself the "happy family." The family that prays together and stays together through sickness and health till death us do part or releases us into the terse joylessness of the epitaphs on our Christian tombstones, erected—for want of any other sort of erection—by those who mourn for us in the curious mode of remembering very hard to forget us very hard. This false mourning is just and poetic, insofar as no authentic mourning is possible if the people who mourn each other have never met each other. The bourgeois nuclear family unit (to use something like the language of its agents —academic sociologists and political scientists) has become, in this century, the ultimately perfected form of nonmeeting, and therefore the ultimate denial of mourning, death, birth and the experiential realm that precedes birth and conception.

Why don't we fall into the welcoming trap, the fur-lined bear trap, of the family's own hypostasization of itself as "The Family," and then explore the various modes in which the infrastructure of the family blocks meeting between any person and any other, and demands a sacrificial offering on the part of each of us that placates no-one and nothing but this highly active abstraction? For want of gods, we have had to invent potent abstractions, none of which are more powerfully destructive than the family.

The power of the family resides in its social mediating function. It reinforces the effective power of the ruling class in any exploitative society by providing a highly controllable paradigmatic form for every social institution. So we find the family form replicated through the social structures of the factory, the union branch, the school (primary and secondary), the university, the business corporation, the church, political parties and governmental apparatus, the armed forces, general and mental hospitals, and so on. There are always good or bad, loved or hated "mothers" and "fathers," older and younger "brothers" and "sisters," defunct and secretly controlling "grandparents." Each of us, in terms of Freud's discovery, transfers bits of our original family experience in the "family of origin" onto each other in our "family of procreation" (our "own" wife and children), and onto each other in whatever situation we work. Then, on this basis of nonreality derived from a prior nonreality, we talk about "people we know," as if we had the remotest chance of knowing the person who knows the people the person supposes himself to know. The family, in other words, as it is socially metamorphosed, anonymizes people who work or live together in any institutional structure; there is an effective seriality, a bus queue, disguised as friendly grouping, in which each "real person" co-operatively works with each other "real person." This exclusion of the reality of the person by internalized figments from his family past is also very well shown by the most basic problem in psychotherapy—the problem of the *progressive depopulation of the room.* At the commencement of therapy the room may hold hundreds of people, principally all the person's family over several generations, but also significant other people. Some of the population inevitably includes the therapist's internalized others—but the guarantee of good therapy is that the therapist is familiar enough with the machinations of his internal family and has them well enough tamed. Bit by bit in therapy, one identifies the members of this vast family and all its extensions and asks them, appropriately enough, to "leave the room," until one is left with two people who are free to meet or leave each other. The ideal end of therapy, then, is the final dissolution of the duality of therapist and "therapeutized"[1]—an illusory state of nonrelation in which therapy, of necessity, has to start and which derives from the family binary role system of bringer-up and brought-up. When will parents allow themselves to be brought up by their children?

1 In French there is no word corresponding to the English word "analysand," implying some sort of development. The only French word for the person on the receiving end of the curative can[ n ]on is *analysé.* The *analysé* really gets it.

It is fatuous to speak of the death of God or the death of Man—parodying the serious intent of certain contemporary theologians and structuralist philosophers—until we can fully envisage *the death of the family*—that system which, as its social obligation, obscurely filters out most of our experience and then deprives our acts of any genuine and generous spontaneity.

Before any cosmic questioning about the nature of God or Man commences, other questions of a more concrete and highly personal type arise, historically, in each of us. "Where have I come from?" "Where did they get me from?" "*Whose* am I?" (One asks this before one can consider asking "*Who* am I?") Then, other less frequently articulated but vaguely suspected questions, such as, "What was happening between my parents before and during my birth?" (i.e., "Did I come from an orgasmic fuck, or what did they think they were doing with each other?"). Or, "Where was I before one of his sperms cracked one of her eggs?" "Where was I before I was I?" "Where was I before I could ask this question where was I before I was this me?"

With a bit of luck one is exceptional (and more of us are exceptional than most of us think if we can remember one or two critical experiences that manifest our exceptionality). Someone, for instance, told me that the midwife who delivered her told her mother: "This one has been here before." More commonly, some people are told that they came from some other parentage: "They made a mistake in the nursing home and got the wrong label on you." This can run, in terms of actual, reported statements, to implications that a certain child comes from another species, that he is clearly nonhuman, or even extraterrestrial and monstrous. One can, however, be so totally conned out of any curiosity that one can internalize a series of unanswered questions as a built-in mystification about one's elemental identity—about who one is, and when, and where one's at. The Family is expert at the self-terrified and self-terrorizing inculcation of the non-necessity of entertaining doubts on any of these points. The Family, since it cannot bear doubt about itself and its capacity to engender "mental health" and "correct attitudes," destroys doubt as a possibility in each of its members.

Each of us are each of its members.

Each of us may have to rediscover the possibility of doubting our origins—despite, and in spite of, being well-brought-up.

I still find myself somewhat incredulous when I meet people who were adopted, or one of whose parents left the home and has never been seen since, and who so deprive themselves of doubt and curiosity that they make no attempt to find the missing parent or parents—not necessarily to have a relationship with them, but simply to witness the fact and quality of their existence. Equally disturbing is the rarity, in fact, of fully developed fantasies about a "romance family" and the sort of ideal and strange family that one might imagine oneself having come from—a family that does not project its problematic[2] onto oneself, but which becomes the imaginary vehicle for one's *own* put-out existence.

In short, one has to reach a position of summing up on one's whole family past; achieving a summing up of all that so as to be free of it in a way that is more personally effective than a simple aggressive rupture or crude acts of geographical separation. If one does it the former way—

2 By "problematic" I mean anything that puzzles or bewilders someone in the present, but which has the prior origin in that person's past in terms not only of family relations but also political structures that get mediated by family, school, etc., to the person.

and this is always through relationships, not necessarily formal, therapeutic relationships—one may attain the rare state of actually liking and being freely fond of one's parents, instead of being engulfed in an imprisoning, ambiguous love—by which, of course, parents are victimized as much as their children.

If we no longer doubt, we become dubious in our own eyes, and can then only opt to lose our vision and see ourselves with the eyes of others—and the eyes of others (each other tormented by the same unrecognized problematic) will see us as duly secure and securing of others. In fact, we become victims of a surfeit of security that eludes doubt, and consequently destroys life in any sense that we can feel alive. Doubt simultaneously freezes and boils the marrow in our bones, it shakes our bones like dice that are never thrown, it plays a secret and violent organ music through the different calibrations of our arteries, it rumbles ominously and affectionately through our bronchial tubes, bladder and bowels. It is, and is the contradiction of, every spermatic contraction, and is the invitation and rejection in every vaginal muscular fluctuation. Doubt, in other words, is real, if we can find our way back to this sort of reality. But if we are to do this, we have to eliminate false routes of athleticism and ritualized yoga—these rituals simply confirm the family plot to externalize bodily experience into something that can be done outside real relationship, and according to a time schedule that reminds one of the toilet training one was bound to submit to in the second year of one's life—or even one's first few months when one was "held out,"[3]—and unminds one of the precise balance between the possibility of evacuating or retaining a certain clearly felt turd.

3 "To be held out" is a British colloquialism meaning to be subjected to compulsive toilet training.

This destruction of doubt sensation and of the experience of living one's body originates in the need for *human grouping*, which is developed first of all in the family. One of the first lessons one is taught in the course of one's family conditioning is that one is not enough to exist in the world on one's own. One is instructed in great detail to disown one's own self and to live agglutinatively, so that one glues bits of other people onto oneself and then proceeds to ignore the difference between the otherness in one's self and the selfsameness of one's self. This is alienation, in the sense of a passive submission to invasion by others, originally the family others. But this passivity is deceptive, insofar as it conceals the active choice to submit to invasion of this sort. All the metaphors of "paranoia" are a poetic protest against this invasion. The poetry, which of course varies in quality, is, however, always unappreciated by society and, if it becomes spoken aloud too much, it gets treated by psychiatry—which is, after educational institutions, the third rung of family defense against autonomy on the part of its members (psychiatry, that is, along with special schools and prisons and a multiplicity of other, more discrete, rejection situations). It seems to me that paranoia in our age—in the first world at least—is a necessary tentative to freedom and wholeness. The only problem is how to be discrete enough to avoid a social assassination or the gentler and more civilized gradual induction of socially acceptable responses by the lengthy psychoanalysis of one's persecutory anxieties. The problem is not to "resolve" the persecutory anxieties but, lucidly, to *use* them to destroy an actual, objective persecutory situation that one is caught up in from even before one's beginnings.

The therapist, in working with people, might far more often have to confirm the reality of paranoid fears than in any sense disconfirm or attempt to modify them. This would no doubt be a projection of the therapist's own paranoia, were it not possible often enough to work out strategies of escaping from, or decisively attacking, the particular sector of the world, with its full persecutory reality, in which the person is immersed and has to ascend out of.

I think, in fact, that what we have to do is to totally revalue certain experiential and behavioral states that are regarded as morbid, and then, through a radical declinicalization of our conceptual framework, see them as more or less abortive or successful strategies to achieve autonomy and self-consistency. In a previous work[4] I have shown the polar opposition, in terms of the truth of a life, between normality (which is the sorry fate of most of us) and sanity and madness, which meet each other at the opposite pole.

The vital point here is the family's role in inducing the base of conformism—normality through the primary socialization of the child. "Bringing up" a child in practice is more like bringing down a person. Education, similarly, is leading a person out of himself and away from himself.

By playing with Greek etymology one may extend this idea.

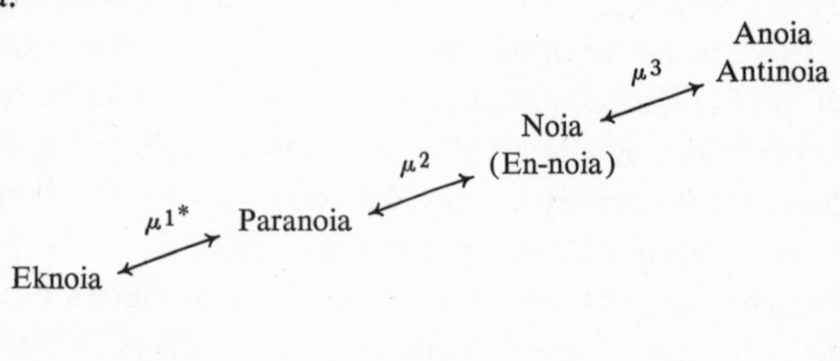


* μ = metanoia

4 *Psychiatry and Antipsychiatry* (New York: Barnes & Noble, 1967; London: Tavistock Publications, 1967).

The eknoid state at the left of the diagram is the normal state of the well-conditioned, endlessly obedient citizen. This is a state of being in which one is so estranged from every aspect of one's own experience, from every spontaneous impulse to action, from every bit of awareness of one's body *for oneself* (rather than one's body as an object for inspection by others in the world), from all the carefully refused possibilities of awakening change, that one might truly, and without metaphorical sleight of hand, regard this normal person as being *out of his mind.* Most people in the first world submit to this chronic murder of their selves with only faintly murmured, fast forgotten dissent. The pay-off for losing one's mind in this sense is of course considerable: one may become affluent, comfortable at least, one may lead a great corporation or a great state, or one may even revel in the ecological devastation of major areas of the earth's surface in the interest of normal values. In fact, on reflection, there's nothing like as good as being out of one's mind. Nor anything like the loss entailed.

By serial metanoias, one may move out of the eknoid position. Metanoia means change from the depths of oneself upward into the superficies of one's social appearance. It includes much of the Pauline sense of conversion and repentance, and, particularly at the second level of metanoia ($\mu 2$), generates the "signs" of depression and mourning. Through the first metanoia one enters a region of "paranoia," of being beside one's self. If eknoia means being out of one's mind, in paranoia one is at least next to one's mind. Paranoia is about a neighborliness of self that might become affectionate. If eknoia is a state of being, a conglomerate of essences that are finally the passive product of social conditioning initiated in the family, paranoia is the beginning of active existence with the possibility of life for new projects. There is certainly confusion between persecutory fantasies and persecutory realities. With the former, one projectively explores social reality through the unknowing, but later half-knowing, superimposition of past experiential structures on the present. If this exploration is radical enough in the context of one's most significant relationships, one begins to develop an objective sense of persecutory reality that is transpersonal and beyond our superimpositions, although indirectly it has been mediated to us by our primary family experience in the first year of life, which conditions the persecutory fantasies.

The second metanoia represents work on one's self in the sense of total work (subsuming the psychoanalytic notion of "working-through") that leads us into a self-consistency, being in our own minds separate as a person from any other person, in unlonely aloneness that is open to the world. Here one encourages one's self, puts a new heart into one's self by invention rather than by transplantation, and one makes a wager to deal with any new experience in the self-containment of one's self-relation, so that one is free to allow a generous issuing of one's self into the world.

At this point one is ready for the abandonment of the self sense, of the restriction to a finite ego. The final metanoia is the fluent *movement between* the actively autonomous self and self (-and world)-transcendence (anoia)—moving through the canceling-out of self–preformation in a moment of anti–noia. There is then, finally, no longer any question of states of being, and the illusory security represented by such states.

There is, of course, much room for confusion of location between these stages, one of the most disastrous being the attempt to move from eknoia and paranoia to anoia without the requisite attainment of self-containing autonomy. The unguided use of psychedelic drugs and abortive, panicky forms of what seem to be "psychotic breakdown" are such attempts. When this happens, people are still very much in the net of the internal family (and often the external family too) and compulsively search for rather less restricting replica family systems.

The family is not only an abstraction, that is, a false existence, an essence, but also exists as a challenge to "go beyond" all the conditioning one has undergone in it. The way one effects this going-beyond seems always to be blocked, however. There are numerous taboos in the family system that reach much further than the incest taboo and taboos against greed and messiness. One of these taboos is the implicit prohibition against experiencing one's aloneness in the world. There seem to be very few mothers indeed who can keep their hands off their child long enough to allow the capacity to be alone to develop. There is always a need to try to arrest the wailing desperation of the other—for one's own sake, not for theirs. This leads to a violation of the temporalization, that is to say the personal time-making as distinct from time-keeping, of the other, so that the mother's need-time system (more or less passively mediating the need-time system of the wider society) gets imposed on the infant's. The infant may need, in *her* or *his* time, to experience frustration, desperation and finally a full-scale experience of depression. In my experience any respect for the time of the other, or the time the other needs to take in their relationship to oneself, is very rare indeed. One of the main, perhaps the most important contributions of Freudian psychoanalytic technique has been the systematic and disciplined development in the analyst of this sort of respect for the natural unfolding of the interplay of temporalizations—without interference, but with total attentiveness. In this sense the psychoanalytic situation can, ideally, become a sort of anti-family—a family that one can enter by choice and leave by choice when one has done what one has to do in it. The analytic situation is not a family transference situation in which one, in some sort of unknowing simplism, converts the other into bits of one's totality of impressions of past family experience. This is only "by the way," although it is a *voie galactique* that one has to traverse. That sort of milk is already spilled, and there is no good in crying over it. So one goes through all this with a proleptic impulse that penetrates one's self with past intimations of the self, that that self would penetrate itself by. What one has to do in it is to discover a fluent dialectic that moves all the time on the shifting antithesis between *being-alone* and *being-with-the-other.* It is this antithesis that we must examine further if we are to discover how a person, deprived of the lifeblood of his solitude in the first year of his life, later, in a moment of great anguish, invents his separateness in the world.

A boy called Philip, at the age of six years, lived with his parents in a hotel owned by relatives. All his life he had been assiduously cared for. He had never been left alone for a moment. But then one day, playing in the gardens, he rested his hands on a white-washed birdbath and looked into the mossy water reflecting the sky. With a shock, he looked up at the sky, seeing it for the first time as if initiated into awareness of its reality by its reflection. Then he realized in a moment of suffocation, which was also a moment of liberation, his total contingency and aloneness in the world. He knew that from that moment onward he could call to no-one, and that no-one could call to him in any way that would deflect the trajectory of his life project, which he now knew he had already chosen—although of course the details would have to be filled in. His mother called out that supper was ready. He went in to eat, but for the first time he knew that he was no longer his mother's child but was, in fact, his own person. The point is that Philip could not say one word about his experience to anyone else in his family that would not be contorted into *their* terms or into some joke about *their* boy.

If one does not discover one's autonomy in one's first year of life, and if one does not discover it by this anguished moment in later childhood, one is either driven mad in late adolescence, or one gives up the ghost and becomes a normal citizen, or one battles one's way through to a freedom in the working out of subsequent relationships, whether these by spontaneously originated or planned, analytic relationships. In any case, one has to leave home one day. Maybe the sooner the better.

This is all about communication and the failure of reception of communication that characterizes the family system. Take a very ordinary situation between parent and child. Parent walks down the high street holding his child's hand. At a certain point there is a necessary breakdown of reciprocity—the parent holds the child's hand, but the child no longer holds the parent's hand. By a subtle kinesic alteration in hand pressure, the child of three or four years indicates to the parent that she wants to make her own way down the high street in her own time. The parent either tightens his grip or takes what he has been taught to experience as a fearful risk—to let his child leave him, not in his time, or in socially prescribed time, but in the child's time.

How do we learn to mind our own business—as did the

Japanese *haiku* poet Bashō? In his journal, *The Narrow Road to the Deep North,* Bashō describes how, shortly after setting out, he saw on the other side of a river an abandoned child, small, desolate and weeping. He could have gone back to the child and found some sort of home for it in a nearby village, but he chose to continue his elected, solitary voyage. Bashō's compassion was fully expressed in verse, but his voyage had to come first—he knew he could do nothing for the child until he knew what he had to do for himself. The hardest lesson of all is to know what one has to do for oneself.

The main task to be accomplished, if we are to liberate ourselves from the family in both the external sense (the family "out there") and the internal sense (the family in our heads), is to *see through* it. To make this phenomenologically real, one might meditate on this visualization—the visualization of a *family queue.* Imagine one looks through a series of veils—the first veil may bear an image of one's mother in a certain mood that one spontaneously remembers, the second veil bears the imprint of one's father in a similar characteristic mood, then one sees through successive veils including siblings, grandparents and all other significant persons in one's life until, at the end of the queue, one sees a veil with one's own image. All one has to do then, having seen through the family, is to see through oneself into a nothingness that returns one to oneself, insofar as this nothingness is the particular nothingness of one's being. After a sufficient view through this nothing, the entailed terror rings with an incidental note only.

To put it another way, the superego (our internalized parents, primitive loved and hated bits and pieces of their bodies, fragments of minatory utterances and confusing life-or-death injunctions that ring through our mental ears from the first year to the last of our lives) has to be transformed from a theoretical abstraction, which we can merely understand, into a phenomenal reality. The superego is *nothing* (the theoretical abstraction) but a series of sensory impressions, images that must be seen, heard, smelled, tasted and touched in our consciousness. For reasons that we may explore later, I shall condense all these sensory modalities into vision, into seeing and seeing through. The object, I think, must be to concretize the superego into real, phenomenal components so that one can *use it* as a sort of social shield, burglar alarm and submachine gun—rather than be used and possibly destroyed by it. The techniques one may find or invent to do this are multifarious.

Apart from interpretations in therapy, one can recall stories and myths and, more importantly, conjure up one's own personal mythology. Lots of us, for instance, talk about the golem myth. Let us remember the original Kabbalistic story. Jewish households erected an effigy of clay and on its brow wrote the word "Aemaeth," meaning "Truth." This monster could be used as a servant doing all manner of household tasks, until it became incompetent or disobedient or simply too big. Then the householder had to reach up to the brow of the golem and erase the first two letters from "Aemaeth"—this left the word "maeth," which meant "he is dead." The monster would then die and be swept away. One householder, however, let the golem grow so big that he could no longer reach the brow of the obstreperous creature. So he thought a bit, and then, knowing that all golems or superegos are essentially obedient, he ordered the creature to bend down and remove his boots. As the golem obeyed him, he erased the first two letters from "Aemaeth"—but forgetting the size of the creature, he was suffocated to death by the mass of original mud that fell onto him. It's all like dying prematurely of coronary thrombosis or cancer or getting shot up by riot police. So how do we befriend our golems—which is all "they" probably want, anyhow.

Then again, to illustrate the power of the internal family, the family that one can separate from over thousands of miles and yet still remain in its clutches and be strangled by those clutches. Someone I saw was trying desperately to free himself from a complex family situation that seemed to invade every move he made in relation to his work and in his relationship with his wife and child. Then one day his mother told him a well-known Jewish story. It was about a young man who fell in love with a beautiful princess in the next town, several miles away. He wanted to marry her, but she made the condition that he would have to cut out the heart of his mother and bring it to her. He went home, and while his mother was sleeping he cut out her heart. Joyously (but secretly only joyfully) he ran back over the fields to the princess, but at one point he stumbled and fell. The heart fell out of his pocket. As he lay there, the heart spoke and asked him, "Have you hurt yourself, my darling son?" By being too obedient to the internal mother, projected in one form into the princess, he became totally enslaved by this internal mother whose omnipresent, immortal love he could never escape again.

Recently a child who had been diagnosed schizophrenic, in "autistic withdrawal," was brought to see me. This beautiful boy of eight was brought into my room by his mother and father, and he wore a badge saying, "It's wrong to eat people." He grimaced and gesticulated and could not (or perhaps more relevantly, did not want to) sit in one place and take part in the discussion. His mother, obviously engaged in some sort of over-eating spree, was consuming the child in terms of an orientation of her whole mind and body to his "welfare"—protecting him from rough friends at school and an overly punitive headmaster who smelled out a "wrong one." But she was erecting this abdominal wall around her son because she was being starved, in terms beyond the sexual, by her husband, who taught at a university west of London. He was starving her because he was being starved of any sort of real intercourse with others by the academic bureaucracy, which mediated to him the first-world famine situation (which seems to be hardly recognized by university administrators, but which is protested with increasing frequency by radical students —with increasing effect). After a few sessions in therapy, in which she got a good feed (talking out, in the mode of drinking in), she tended to "eat up" her son less and less. He went back to school and formed his first friendships with other boys. A month later I saw him again, and this time he bore none of the psychiatric stigmata—this time he wore a badge saying, "Eat me up, I'm delicious." The "clinical problem" was resolved. Beyond that there is only politics.

A Tibetan monk, engaged in a long solitary meditative withdrawal, began to hallucinate a spider. Every day the spider appeared, growing larger each time, until finally it was as big as the man himself and appeared very threatening. At this point the monk asked his guru for advice and obtained the following: "Next time the spider comes, draw a cross on its belly and then, with due reflection, take a knife and plunge it into the middle of the cross." The next day the monk saw the spider, drew the cross and then reflected. Just as he was about to plunge the knife into the spider's belly, he looked down and in amazement saw the mark chalked across his own umbilicus. It is evident that to distinguish between the inner and the outer adversary is literally a matter of life or death. The spider was the internal family that could only harm him in fantasy.

Families are about the inner and the outer.

Families are about life or death or ignominious flight.

One very obvious manifestation of the operation of unseen, or insufficiently seen, internalized family structures is in political demonstrations where the organizing group is lacking in vision of this sort of reality in themselves. So we find demonstrators getting unnecessarily hurt because they unknowingly project bits of their parents in their negative, punishing, powerful aspect onto the police. This leads to an attack "from the rear," insofar as they are defending themselves not only against the attack from the police "out there" but also against the internal attack from the family policeman in their heads. The *people* most vulnerable to this twofold attack are, significantly, smelled out by the police and the judges; significantly those demonstrators who dutifully get beaten up most severely also get the heaviest sentences in the courts. The revolutionary objective is, needless to say, forgotten.

If we are to regard paranoia as a morbid state of existence in any sense any more, I think that the only place in which we find this as a social problem is in the minds of policemen, administrators of the law, and the consensus politicians of the imperialist countries. These unfortunate people embody the projected superegos of the rest of us to such an extent that their internalizations of the self-punitive bits of our minds squeeze them out of any sort of human existence of their own. Any compassion that *we* achieve in relation to *them*, however, need not stultify the effective force of our anger against the real persecution unknowingly embodied by them—against the third world that is situated in Africa, Asia and Latin America as well as against the unrecognized and self-unrecognizing third world that resides in the heart of the first world. I shall define this secret third world later—for the moment, suffice it to say that it is black (whatever one's literal color), hippy, orientated to local seizure of power in factories, universities, schools. It's deprived not *of* education but *by* education, it breaks the cannabis laws and more often than not gets away with it, and it knows how to burn cars and make bombs that sometimes work. This secret third world gets put down as suffering, for instance, from "infantile omnipotence"—a malady which, one psychiatric colleague suggested, afflicted the Red Guards in the Cultural Revolution. The emerging question, however, is whether this so-called psychopathological category may now elude the amateur diagnostics of the family and some of their psychiatric colleagues, all of whom are so imbued with the frightened archaeo-ideology of the bourgeois watchdog that in terror would evade its reality as a lapdog. Having eluded this invalid possibility, the people so stigmatized may find a social revolutionary use for their "aberrations" instead of letting them sink into a private neurosis which always confirms "the system" and plays endless, joyless games with it.

Through considerations of this sort, one begins to sense a rumbling, deep-toned possibility asserting itself—perhaps fearfully, certainly terrorizing in its intent: the possibility of a destructuring of the family on the basis of a full realization of the destructiveness of that institution. A destructuring that will be so radical—precisely because of the lucidity that finally points the way to it—that it demands a revolution in the whole society. All the time now we have to differentiate between prerevolutionary and postrevolutionary forms and possibilities. In concrete terms, all we can do in a prerevolutionary context is to lay down certain isolated prototypes that may be developed on a mass social scale in a postrevolutionary context.

Let us sum up on some of the factors that operate within the family, often with lethal but always with humanly stultifying consequences. Later we shall explore the possibilities of reversing them.

Firstly, there is the gluing together of people based on the sense of one's own incompleteness. To take one classical form of this, let us consider the mother who feels incomplete as a person (owing to a complex set of reasons that usually includes, with contrality, her relationship with her mother, and the general suppression of extrafamilial social effectiveness in women). So in the whole colloidal system of the family she glues, say, her son onto herself, to be that bit of her self that she feels to be missing (the bit her mother "taught" her was missing) and the bit that actually is missing (the factor of objective social suppression). The son, even if he "succeeds" in leaving home and getting married, may never become more personally complete than her, because he has experienced himself during the most critical years of his "formation" as an appendage to her body—(her penis)—and to her mind—her mind-penis, or socially prescribed effectiveness. In the most extreme form of this symbiosis, his only exit might be by a series of acts that lead him to be designated schizophrenic (about one percent of the population are hospitalized at some point in their lives with this label), and transferred to the replica family of the mental hospital. Probably the only way that people, glued to each other in the family and in the replica families of social institutions, can unglue themselves is by using the warmth of love. The irony here is that love gets warm enough to accomplish this ungluing only if it traverses a region usually experienced as arctic: the region of total respect for one's own autonomy and for that of each other person one knows.

Secondly, the family specializes in the formation of roles

for its members rather than in the laying down of conditions for the free assumption of identity. I do not mean identity in the congealed, essentialist[5] sense, but rather a freely changing, wondering but highly active sense of who one is. Characteristically, in a family a child is indoctrinated with the desired desire to become a certain sort of son or daughter (then husband, wife, father, mother), with a totally enjoined, minutely prescribed "freedom" to move within the narrow interstices of a rigid lattice of relationship. Instead of the feared possibility of acting from the chosen and self-invented center of oneself, being *self-centered* in a good sense, one is taught to submit, or else, to live in an eccentric way of being in the world. Here, "eccentric" means being normal or located in the normal—way off the center of oneself, which becomes a forgotten region from which only our dream voices address us, in a language that we have equally forgotten. Most of our conscious use of language amounts to little more than a pale, squeaking facsimile of the strange, deeper-resonating tongues of our dreams and prereflective modes of awareness ("unconscious").

Being a well-brought-up, eccentric, normal person means that one lives all the time relatively to others, and this is how the falsely splitting system originates in family indoctrination, so that one functions all the time in social groups in later life as one side or other of a duality. Essentially, this is collusion on the parameter,[6] refusal/acceptance, of one's freedom. One refuses certain possibilities of one's own and deposits these refused possibilities in the other, who in turn deposits his possibilities of an opposite

5 By "essentialist" I mean the interposition across the line of one's vision of general categories of thought that make it difficult to see the concrete individual being.

6 By "parameter" I mean implicity or explicity defined lines of argument about where a person is at in relation to each other person in a situation of meeting.

sort in oneself. In the family there is the built-in antithesis of the bringer-up (parents) and the brought-up (children). All possibilities of children bringing up their parents are relegated. The socially imposed "duty" of parents suppresses, finally, any joy that might shatter the division of roles. This obligation structure is then transported into every other institutional system subsequently entered by the person brought up in the family (I include, of course, adoptive families and orphanages, which follow the same model). One of the saddest scenes I know is when a child of six or seven plays school with desks and lessons arranged, under the parents' view, in precisely the same form that exists in the primary school. How might we reverse this abdication, and stop stopping the child teaching her or his secret wisdom that we make them forget because we forget that we have forgotten it?

Thirdly, the family, in its function as primary socializer of the child, instills social controls in its children that are patently more than the child needs to navigate his way through the obstacle race laid down by the extrafamilial agents of the bourgeois state, whether these be police, university administrators, psychiatrists, social workers, or his "own" family that passively re-creates his parents' family model—although the television programs these days are a bit different, of course. The child, in fact, is taught primarily not how to survive in society but how to submit to it. Surface rituals like etiquette, organized games, mechanical learning operations at school replace deep experiences of spontaneous creativity, inventive play, freely developing fantasies and dreams. These forms of life have to be systematically suppressed and forgotten and replaced by the surface rituals. It may take therapy, in the best sense, to revalue one's experience highly enough to register one's dreams properly, and to sequentially develop one's dreams beyond the point of dream stagnation that most people reach before the age of ten. If this happens on a wide enough scale, therapy becomes dangerous to the bourgeois state and highly subversive because radically new forms of social life are indicated. Suffice it to say for the moment, however, that every child, before family indoctrination passes a certain point and primary school indoctrination begins, is, germinally at least, an artist, a visionary and a revolutionary. How do we recover this lost potential, how do we start stepping backward on the inexorable march from the truly *ludic,* joyful play that invents its autonomous discipline, to the *ludicrous*—that is, normal, games-playing social behavior, obedient to a narrow set of rules?

Fourthly, and this again we shall explore in subsequent chapters, there is an elaborate system of taboos that is instilled in each child by its family. This, like the teaching of social controls more generally, is achieved by the implantation of guilt—the sword of Damocles that will descend on the head of anyone who prefers his own choices and his own experiences to those enjoined on him by the family and the wider society. If one loses one's head enough to openly disobey these injunctive systems, one is, poetically enough, decapitated! The "castration complex," far from being morbid, is a social necessity for bourgeois society, and it is when they are in danger of *losing* it that many people, in perplexity, search for therapy—or a new form of revolution.

The taboo system that the family teaches extends well beyond the obvious incest taboos. There is a restriction of the sensory modalities of communication between people to the audio-visual, with quite marked taboos against people in the family touching, smelling or tasting each other. Children may romp with their parents, but demarcation lines are very firmly drawn around the erotogenic zones on both sides. There has to be a very carefully measured obliquity and stiltedness in, say, the way that growing-up sons have to kiss their mothers. Transexual hugging and holding are rapidly precipitated, in the minds of family members, into a zone of "dangerous" sexuality. Above all, there is the taboo on tenderness that Ian Suttie (in *Origins of Love and Hate*) wrote so well about. Tenderness in families may be felt, certainly, but not expressed unless it is formalized almost out of existence. One is reminded of the young man, quoted by Grace Stuart,[7] who, on seeing his father in his coffin, bent over him and kissed his brow, saying, "There, father, I never dared do that while you were alive!" Perhaps if we realized how dead "alive" people are we might be prepared, goaded by despair, to take more of a risk.

Throughout this chapter I have, perforce, used a language that I find archaic, essentially reactionary and certainly discrepant with my thinking. Family words like "mother," "father," "child" (in the sense of "their" child), "superego." The connotation of "mother" takes in a number of biological functions, primary protector functions, a socially overdefined role and a certain legal "reality." In fact, the maternal function can be diffused into other people beyond the mother: the father, siblings, and above all, other people outside the biologically grouped family. There seems to me to be no sense in reducing complex but intelligible social relationships to purely contingent and circumstantial biological facts—facts that are mere facts, facts that precede acts which initiate a true sociality. I remember a conjoint session with a mother and her daugh-

7 Grace Stuart, *Narcissus, A Psychological Study of Self-Love* (New York: Macmillan, 1955; London: George Allen and Unwin Ltd., 1951).

ter described to me by a colleague. At one point the mother, with deep sadness and not a little courage, said that she had begun to feel a tremendous and decisive sense of loss and envy on realizing that the therapist (a man) was now her daughter's mother far more than she was. The boundary between "transference" relationship and "real" relationship can never be—and I believe never should be—all that clear. It's a matter of living a necessary ambiguity, with a requisite sense of difference between the projected (altering) image and the unaltered perception of the other.

Anyhow, with this grumble against the language one has to use, I shall not suggest a new language now but simply underline the fatuity and danger of the fetish of consanguinity.

Blood is thicker than water only in the sense of being the vitalizing stream of a certain social stupidity.

The family, for want of a capacity for producing holy Idiots, becomes moronic.

# The Topography of Love

In the Nuremberg War-Crime Trials a witness appeared who had lived for a time in a grave in a Jewish graveyard, in Wilna, Poland. It was the only place that he—and many others—could live, when in hiding after they had escaped the gas chamber. During this time he wrote poetry; one of the poems was a description of a birth. In a grave nearby a young woman gave birth to a boy. The eighty-year-old gravedigger, wrapped in a linen shroud, assisted. When the new-born child uttered his first cry, the old man prayed: "Great God, hast Thou finally sent the Messiah to us? For who else than the Messiah Himself can be born in a grave?" But after three days the poet saw the child sucking his mother's tears because she had no milk for him.[8]

I THINK THAT in talking about the family and marriage we have to play tricks with language until finally we generate a certain vertigo in ourselves through which words, falsely assumed to transmit knowledge, lose their apparent meaning, and a more real discourse is possible—implying ultimately the invention of a new language,

8 Paul Tillich, *The Shaking of the Foundations* (New York: Scribner, 1948, p. 165; Harmondsworth, Middlesex: Pelican, 1962).

a language that does not only have to be spoken and written.[9] In the future I believe books will never be written again, books will be *done*, thus literalizing the clichéd metaphor that writing is an act.

All verbal language is impositional in a way that nonverbal communication is not. The weight of assumed meaning in words is considerably more than in the case of, say, paralinguistic and kinesic modes of expression, where ritual runs surface-deep only. The assumed meaning is twofold: in the first place it is derived from the past, accumulated connotation of each word, and secondly, from the writer or speaker's present, syntactical deployment of each word.

So one tricks words, because if one does not one will be tricked by them. As is the case with all institutionalized systems, one has to counterplay the system's game; firstly, to elude it in personal terms, secondly, to transcend it in historical terms. Now, as regards talking about the topography of love, that is to say, where love is at—if anywhere—today, I shall take, as a paradigmatic case, the word "marriage."

Beyond the obvious legal and social-contractual senses of the word, marriage can mean any sort of more or less lasting, socially objectified conjunction between personal entities. If we recognize that each of us is filled with a world of others who are not quite *them* and at the same time not quite *us*, we can envisage the possibility of some marital arrangement *within one person.* If we go back in the tradition of phenomenological investigation of human

9 One reflects on the difference in historical effect of the written and the oral Torah. The former became a humanly restricting but socially cohering teaching; the latter, transmitted by face-to-face confrontation situations in which every small gesture and intonation became part of the message, became a dangerous source of joy and liberation that all the time had to be drawn back into the verbal capsule.

experience, we recall the definition of intentionality running through the work of Husserl and Sartre, in particular. Any primary datum of experience arising as a thinking, feeling, striving movement is *of* something, towards some object that both constitutes and is constituted by the initial movement in consciousness as a unitary and self-uniting entity in the world.

At this point we have to deviate because we cannot talk about marriage without talking about love, and we cannot talk about love without talking about instinct. Probably, in the psychoanalytical literature, the most dubious and obscure verbal entity is "instinct" or, worse, the "instinctual drive." So far, the use of this term has been little more than a deceptive aid to theoretical writing, something that has unfortunately made writing possible when a historic act of waiting and silence might have been more appropriate. In the whole field of its usage it is the violent inruption of pure abstraction into almost any concrete experience of need and desire. I would suggest that the word "instinct" might disappear into a unity that has been falsely split up, although of course in the way one has to talk about it now, one can only reflect on the split.

If we talk about an instinctual urge to have a good feed, we are talking about something that comes from nothing. Something may come from nothing if the nothing is a particular nothing. In this case the particularity of the nothing is the line of its circumscription by the world as an absence—a lack, what is not there. The world here includes certain edible objects, the distance and obstacles between us and the objects, and our bodies as objects in the world that can be observed by others, for example, the hunger contractions in our stomachs, the neurochemical alterations in the hunger state that can be recorded, and so on. It's a bit like running one's finger across a table and then letting it drop off into nothing at the edge. The edge is neither the table nor is it the "nothing" one's finger drops into, but both the table, which is something, and the nothing, which is not, define the edge as nonexistent, but as a specific nonexistence. If we can extend our metaphysical imagination to the point of desubstantializing our finger, so that it becomes a nonfinger, we get closer to what an instinct "is."

But then one must go further, and I think go further in this direction: there is, I would maintain, no logically justifiable distinction, and certainly no real distinction *in experience* (until we begin to be analytic and fragmenting in relation to our experience), between the "instinctual urge" and its object. Of course, as I have said, the language one has to use about this betrays the realization, but let us say just this: the instinctual urge that carries us in the direction of a good feed *is nothing less than the good feed itself in its full significance.* This is true, however, as we shall see, in terms of a lying antithesis, of "both" the "external" dinner on our plate "and" the "internal" good breast (which of course is one condensed way of expressing a myriad of appetitively fulfilling internal images). The phrase "instinctual gratification" means simply the coalescing consciousness of the inner and the outer object, and this in turn means a decisive dissolution of the experienced boundary of one's self. Ungratified instinct is the experience of being poised on the boundary of one's self, frightened of the precariousness of this position but, even more, unable to relinquish the security of a clearly felt, egoic consciousness. One man in this position had a dream in which he was running, carrying his self in a teaspoon.

In talking about instinct I have deliberately chosen an oral situation first, because a genital-sexual-instinctual-situation might, deceptively, seem too simple. It is commonplace now to speak of the death experience of orgasm and the loss of self-boundaries in that state. The threat of instinctual gratification is, I think, more striking in the oral case. This threat assumes the proportions it does because, of course, it is an ontological ultimate. Instinctual fulfillment means, in every instance, the breakdown of self-boundaries, and thus becomes an equivalent to madness, if not madness itself. If, then, we wish to find the most basic level of understanding of repression in society, we have to see it as a collectively reinforced and institutionally formalized panic about going mad, about the invasion of the outer by the inner and of the inner by the outer, about the loss of the illusion of "self."

The Law is terror put into words.

Because of the terror, the words have to be deprived of any personal reference.

Because of the terror, anyone who is no-one judges no-one who might be anyone. Because of the abstract nature of the judgment, the crime becomes abstract. So that courts and prisons and all our institutions may go on. So all that remains is suffering—in no-one, about nothing. The unlocatability of suffering is what we suffer from. And this is true of all of us. All the judges and all their victims. The actual suffering of the punished person is an arbitrary, gratuitous fact, thrown into the world to lend false substantiality to an etheric system.

The bourgeois state is a tranquilizer pill with lethal side effects.

The socio-historical understanding of repression has been impressively worked out; what we now have to do is to reflect on, and act from, a realization of its ontological infrastructure.[10]

10 I am not disputing the classical Marxist distinction between the infrastructure as materiality (in the sense of means of production and relations of production interacting and interpenetrating with the suprastructure, which is

Staying awhile with the oral case, let us consider phenomena such as the hallucinated good breast of the infant and transitional objects, e.g., the favorite rag of a little girl. These are usually taken to mean a sort of grudging or half-protesting movement towards "reality." Of course (perhaps with analytic help) one gets beyond all this, and it joins the rest of our duly resolved, unconscious baggage in the left-luggage office of our minds. But what if the protest becomes less halfhearted and we cease to equate the resolution of conflict with adequate social adjustment? What if the hallucinated good breast is an attempt to maintain a transpersonal identity of the inner and the outer, the one successful moment of madness that most of us have, and have to lose all sight of very quickly? What if the corner of the rag that the little girl sucks is more real than her mother's breast (which "is" the breast she *no longer* sucks) or the internal good breast that she projects into the rag? Can we not conceive of a sense in which the rag as what it is in fact—neither subjective nor objective (that is to say, neither inner nor outer good breast)—comes first? In other words, the search of the little girl for the right corner of the rag is not in the little girl, nor between her and the rag, nor anywhere else in the world but in the rag itself. The rag itself is constituted as a breast substitute by the child, but this is a false hermeneutic, insofar as it is a nonreciprocal explanation that comforts, primarily, only the explainer (although, of course, as is true of much heavily interpretative psychotherapy, the child may derive a certain comfort from the feeling that at least the explainer is explaining something to himself). The world in this sense is full of miraculous objects that precede the

consciousness), and its products, which "reflect" the infrastructure. By ontological infrastructure I mean the *source* of the interaction and interpenetration, the unanalyzable but locatable precondition of analysis.

person who witnesses or makes miracles. The man who *talks* of magic is superfluous.

The only point in being born is to discover that "one" already has been.

> The only point in dying is to experience *this* fact of one's birth.
> This point is the geometric point.
> Geometry is hard work.

After these considerations of the relation of the inner to the outer and of both of these to what is neither, let us return to love and marriage—if for a while we can support this particular conjunction of terms.

From some partly assumed, partly appointed locus in the world, one has to see through one's family into the inviting but somewhat murky world of other people outside it. One has to see through one's parents' marriage and one's own state of, in some sense, being married to their marriage and one's own marriage to each of one's parents in turn. Also, one's marriage to each of one's siblings and to each of the "other significant persons" (and to their marriage to oneself, since marriage can be entirely nonreciprocal—one can feel married to someone who does not feel married to oneself). Then, before one arrives at any marital relationship with other people in the world outside one's family, one has to go through a whole lot of divorce proceedings with each of these people to a more or less partial or total degree. One may finally have to get divorced from one's relationship with one of one's parents, or divorced from one's infatuation with their marriage, and so on, seriatim, through the sibling ranks and the ranks of "significant others."

After one has gone through this more or less successfully, one is left on one's own ready to face the possibility of marriage yet once again, with someone else from outside the system, but no doubt within their own comparable if not identical system.

Ultimately, to avoid going through endless repetitions of what one has already gone through (but using new, i.e., unoriginal, other people instead of the original other people, i.e., the even less original others of one's family), one might decide on a return to oneself—and then to see what sort of relationship one might wish to have with oneself. One may further marry oneself or get further divorced from oneself, and maybe divorce and estrangement from oneself are not quite the same thing. So one retraces one's steps and reaches a point of either hating oneself enough to generate yet another repetition of the ancient scheme of half-made-up minds and lives, or of loving oneself enough —through a serial divorce from the relationships of all other half-married, half-divorced people in one's mind—in order to meet oneself fully enough, and then decide what, if anything, one wants to do with oneself in relation to all these other relationship possibilities.

One may attain a point of sufficient "narcissism" to re-evaluate that "psychopathological" category in the direction of a realization that one can never love another person until one can love oneself enough, on every level, including the level of proper (i.e., full, orgasmic) masturbation—that is, masturbating at least once with joy. And further, each should be able to masturbate in the full vision of the other. Without a secure enough base in self-love, one inevitably and repetitively acts out the whole mass of implanted guilt in one's relations with others.

In the earlier part of this century, mental hospitals in England supplied their staff with a large poster listing the causes of mental disease. Prominent at the head of this list was masturbation. The progress of liberal psychiatry has made this attribution seem ridiculous, but this is simply to displace a lie with another lie. Of course masturbation drives people mad, if one begins to see it as a form of sexuality that denies the family one has to prepare oneself to set up, if it is seen as a denial of the socially desired loss of oneself into otherness—but above all if one masturbates *properly*, that is to say in the sense of a limitless exploration of one's own body, including every form of "antisocial" withdrawal that might be entailed by this anti-epistemology of carnal knowledge of one's self that moves towards the other *when it is ready*.

I think it worthwhile at this point to distinguish between a loving relationship and a love relationship, although we may always hope for a merging of the two. A loving relationship is a relationship in which each person makes it possible for the other to love herself, or himself, enough to precondition a development of the relationship. It's all a matter of how one doesn't stop the other person from being *nice* and *kind* to herself or himself. These phrases are banal to the point of emotional idiocy, but we may have to become emotional idiots with a full respect of this need, first in ourselves and then in the other. My experience has been that one can do no good work with a group until one can preconditionally catalyze the possibility of being nice and kind to each other. This always takes time and it takes work. But then to love we have, perhaps, to sweat out the disillusionment of love.

Let us try to put this in slightly different terms.

Why not gamble and "play the system" quite seriously in this sense? Let us talk about marriage as something real, a conjunction between people or between people and the opposites of themselves. In this sense we are internally polygamous to quite a remarkable extent. What we leave out, significantly, is our secret, and secreted, marriage to ourselves. So, the internal constellation looks somewhat like this:

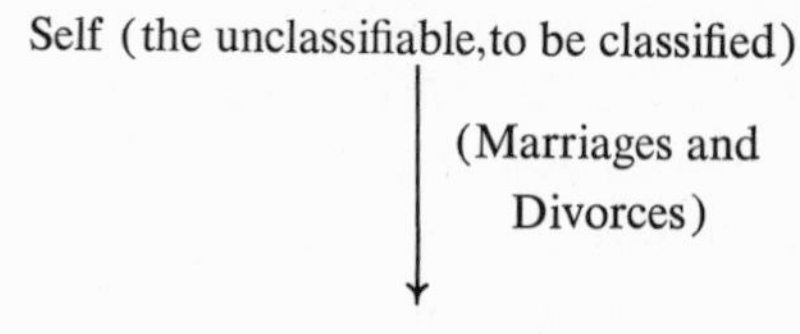


Grand- and great-grandparents, mother, father, brothers, sisters, sons, daughters, grand- and great-grandsons and daughters and all the most cousinly and auntly and unclely extensions of this system

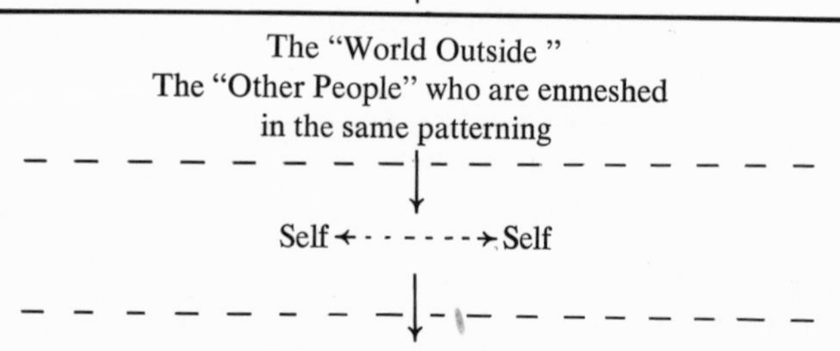


"That's where we came in," but could not come.

The usual state of affairs here is that the self haltingly gropes through the family world, both inside and outside his mind, and then stumbles into the world outside the family. The world outside the family, he finds, tries to make itself as much like the family world he has known before as it can, just as the family world tried to make itself as much like the world outside as it could. There seems to be no worthwhile difference between the two, unless the self, the person, can invent such a difference. If the person realizes this, that in fact the essence of being a boring person is not to have gone beyond, in imagination at least, the limited horizons of one's family and to repeat or collude with repetitions of this restrictive system outside the family, that, in short, *to be a boring person is to be a family person, a person who finds the primacy of her or his existence in the mirror reflection rather than in the mirrored,* then the person may go back to where he started and try to meet himself, court himself, and marry himself.

Of course when the person returns to his self, his line of vision is distorted by serial refractions through others: first outside and then inside his family, and all the time through the others, inside as well as outside his mind (a sense of difference, if not a defining awareness, is always there). Finally, however, when this project has been accomplished, the self meets himself in a deserted inner world—where all the others have shriveled up from the irradiation effects of his spirit—and he wanders alone in the wasteland, finding sustenance in the stone he sucks and the ash ingested by the pores of his skin.

Then, if he wants an oasis, he will form one between the mounds of his sand with the tears he secretes. Then, he might invite another to come to him for sustenance and to sustain him. But he will always remain in his desert because this is his freedom. If one day he no longer needs his freedom, then this is his freedom also. But in any case, the desert remains.

If we attempt to look at the expression of love as a social fact, one social reaction becomes dominant in the whole field of responses—the reaction of hatred. The appearance of love is subversive to any good social ordering of our lives. Far more than being statistically abnormal, love is dangerous, it might even spread through the aseptic shield that we each get each other to erect around ourselves. What we are socially conditioned to need and expect is not love, but security. Security means the full and repeatedly reinforced affirmation of the family. A man marries a woman whom he will never leave, and because she knows that he will never leave her, she will never leave him. She accepts the conditionality of her situation because there is a social bribe built into it, in the sense that her husband can only opt out of the conditional system if he, as the apparent initiator of the whole scene, accepts guilt that may be lethal or nearly lethal to him. So he suffers, this poor man, at least until at last the penny drops, and he sees through the megalomania that he has been so well instructed in and sees his own pay-off in terms of the capacity to feel endlessly guilty and to lacerate himself with this alien guilt.

A man in his late thirties, married with four children, once told me this story. One night, not having taken alcohol or any other drug, he awakened at 3 A.M. He had been in a dreamless sleep until he suddenly awakened to a startling realization about what he thought to be the meaning of his whole life. At first it seemed very gentle, a gradual silting up of the blood in the small vessels at the extremities of his body. It started under his fingernails and toenails and in the lobes of his ears and the tip of his nose. Then it spread as an ominous clotting through all the major blood vessels of his body. At each moment he felt he might cancel out the experience by disappearing—flying off from his fingertips, dropping off from the tip of his nose. The capillaries in his brain filled with coagulating blood, and one by one his cortical neurons died; just enough were left for a consciousness of his heart. Then his coronary arteries clotted up, until his heart stopped, died, and then burst into a huge galactic ejaculation that spread throughout the cosmos. In that moment of universal dissemination, he experienced a melting away of every bit of anger and resentment to anyone that he had ever experienced. It was all pure love and beyond love, compassion, until he told his wife of the experience later in the morning. He had been through a death-and-rebirth experience, he knew at last the meaning of compassion, there need no longer be any problems that really mattered between them.

But how she hated him for that. And how right she was. The social collective exists, after all, and as long as we need it to exist as a collective, we will need families that define love as subversive to security and normality. And we will also need all bluffs to be called.

The tragedy in this case was nothing less than the fate of being married, of having one's relationship defined, not in an interior way, which would allow the possibility of indiscrete personal revelation, but from the outside, in a manner that proscribes the utterance of truth—or else "it all breaks up."

Only, even if it does, it never does. Merely divorce may happen.

In an almost naive way, it always seems strange and ironic to me that people cannot dare speak *their* truth, however distorted their perspective in this respect, in the relationship of marriage in any sense of the latter term, whether legally confirmed or based more straightforwardly on agreement and understanding between two people who want to love together, with or without other people, such as children, coming into the ménage. People would rather go to the heavily stereotyped, complex figure called the psychotherapist, whom one pays by the hour, who has the full nature of the prostitute (being all things for anyone)—often without the honesty of realizing his vocation—but to whom one can trust one's experiences, although not too optimistically, on the level of death and rebirth.

With regard to "problems" such as narcissism and homosexuality, it seems to me that psychoanalytic theory is overburdened with puritanical doubts about these states.

We can, I think, reduce this complex region to one very simple statement that need no longer be implied but rather directly expressed, as follows.

One can no longer think of loving another person until

one can love oneself enough. Love of oneself here means a full realization of one's body: both its outside folds and creases and fullness, its dark and light zones, and also the full experience of the insides of one's body—one has to know the fluctuations of one's bowel musculature, the sound of ureteral dripping into one's bladder, the blood in each ventricle of one's heart. Then, with a quasi-objectivity, having studied one's body like a physiologist, one can break down the compartmentalization of it into a gesture that means self-love. One has to get fully enough into the full erectile-ejaculatory sense of one's clitoris or penis.

Before one can love another, one has to love oneself enough. Before one can love another of the opposite sex, one has to be able to love another/others of the same sex "enough." Whether one overtly lives out one's homosexuality or not is immaterial, but it is certain that one has to recognize its inruptions into one's fantasies[11] and dreams—even into the fantasies a man has with the woman he loves, but even more (because of the prevalent supression of the full sexuality of women,) into the fantasies between the woman and the man whom she loves.

In fact, narcissism and homosexuality are no more diseases or fixated states of development than are phenomena such as holding down a steady job, duly providing for one's family, or, in general, being a pillar of society. The real problem for the therapist arises when people sink and drown in the latter state.

11 I mean here fantasies as conscious meditations and not fantasy in the sense of "unconscious fantasy," i.e., the "projection" of the "interiorized," and "re-introjection" of the "projection."

# The Two Faces of Revolution

BEFORE TALKING about new types of living arrangements between people that may avoid the restrictions and subtle violence of the family, one point has to be made clear first. In the case of the capitalist countries of the first world, one can only talk about communes as prototype situations that can never freely extend and flourish in a prerevolutionary context. The psychology of appropriation, of treating other people—to a greater or lesser extent—as commodities that one may possess or exchange, is so objectively prevalent that instances of the transcendence of it must be rare and isolated. Even in these rare cases the transcendence is usually more apparent than real, insofar as there seems to be an inevitable resort to suppression (trying not to think), repression, denial (the "unconscious" or prereflective maneuvers), and various strategies of withdrawal. By these various means, we can evade the spectacle of our possessing and "using" other people—usually, of course, in the form of a collusion, since people are so conditioned to be used and exploited in relationships.

What we have to do in this first-world context is to accumulate experience in the prerevolutionary situation that can achieve full social expression only after revolution —which I believe has to be strategically reconsidered in the first world, and reconsidered precisely on the ground of micropolitical experience, that is, the experience gained in groups that range from the two-person meeting to any meeting between people that is not so large that people cannot achieve a full internalization of each other that leads to a clear sense of recognition and of being recognized, whatever confusion about the "exact" identity of each other remains in peoples' minds.[12]

In this chapter I shall refer to certain forms of commune arrangement that have been attempted in the first world, but will not consider types of anti-family arrangement that have been worked out, particularly in Cuba and China. The parallels between first-world countries and revolutionary, third-world countries are very few indeed, until we define further the meaning of a hidden third world in the heart of the first world. Before proceeding, however, let me define the "commune" as a potential alternative form of microsocial organization in the first world. A commune is a microsocial structure that achieves a viable dialectic between solitude and being-with-others; it implies either a common residence for the members, or at least a common work and experience area, around which residential situations may spread out peripherally; it means that love relationships become diffused between members of the commune network far more than is the case with the family system, and this means, of course, that sexual relationships are not restricted to some socially approved two-

12 E.g., in one therapeutic community I know, people are supposed to "get to know" each other by announcing their names and work background, seriatim.

person, man-woman arrangement; above all, because this strikes most centrally at repression, it means that children should have totally free access to adults beyond their biological parental couple. These definitional elements point to an ideological *prise de position* that one may state thus: *making love is good in itself, and the more it happens in any way possible or conceivable between as many people as possible, the better.*

But let me retrench for a while from this position to register certain provisos. I think that the minimum condition for a relationship between people to be a love relationship is the experience, after a great deal of relationship work, of tenderness—which is the positive residue of feeling after all negativity, resentment, hostility, envy and jealousy have been dissolved away frequently enough and deeply enough. If one tightens one's definition of love considerably, this feeling amounts to trust. This means an end to secrets, no relationship act carried out behind anyone else's back, although privacy, antithetic to family-modeled secrecy, always remains a possibility. But let us not fall into some sort of euphoric myth about openness at this point. Openness, in the sense I am suggesting here, means a lot of hard work. What I am suggesting means, inevitably, a considerable amount of suffering from the consequences of emotional mistakes one makes in one's relationships, and a disciplined, even ruthless clarification of blocks and compulsions that operate within one's mind. Openness means pain, and, despite attentive kindness and help and clarification that one may get from other people, the pain ultimately has to be suffered alone. It is from this position of solitude that the ultimate clarification must come. Make no mistake about it, other people will always sense, even without realizing what they sense, when someone in the group has been through this sort of self-confrontation. It would be fatuous to speak of communes without the presence in the group of, in the first instance, at least one person who has rigorously enough dealt with his life in these terms.

This leads on very naturally to a consideration of jealousy, the major point on which commune arrangements tend to break down. Jealousy, classically, seems to be triadic in its structure. Person A is jealous of person C, who is having a relationship with person B who, in person A's eyes, is "his" person. Now I do not think that the triadic structure here is the most troublesome aspect of the jealousy situation. We know, of course, that a lot of the fear and the ensuing anger in person A derives from his repressed homosexual wishes, directed in this case to person C, so that when person C penetrates person B genitally, this is a wished-for and terrifying anal rape of person A (to take a straightforward heterosexual example, with male jealousy as the active force). This aspect would be dealt with ideally in the commune by A, and for that matter by C and B: all three would become aware of their repressed homosexuality so that, for instance, A and C could have a good or at least clearly seen relationship between themselves. (This might involve an overt sexual relationship, but whether sexuality is explicitly or implicitly recognized is simply an indifferent matter of choice and predilection —homosexuality in this case, or any form of sexuality in any case, should be an open possibility, never a duty!)

There is, however, a more elusive level of the understanding of jealousy that seems to me to be if anything monadic rather than triadic. One of the worst fates of a two-person relationship, and this is above all true of many marital relationships during most of their history, is that the two people enter into a symbiotic relationship with each other, so that each becomes the other's parasite, each becomes hidden in the inside of the other's mind. One looks for person A and finds him in the mind of person B, but person B is inside the mind of person A, and so on through serial internalizations by each of the others' internalizations of their internalizations of the other, and so on. In this way both A and B become invisible, with all the imperturbability and security of social invisibility. This is really "happy marriage," the price being simply a disappearance of one's human being. So persons A and B disappear into a composite personal entity A-B. Then person C comes along, but C is only an *apparent* third, since A and B are more really one than two persons. In this case C, an illusory person, has a "relationship" with B who, as B, is of course also illusory. A then becomes disturbed by C's "relationship" with B, but "jealousy," in this case, means that A sees himself with C's eyes (that is to say, C is really A looking at A: the violence by which A and B have eliminated their separate realities extends to C, who ceases to be himself, whoever he was, and unwittingly becomes a hitherto refused self-reflective embodiment of A). The issue here is the sudden fracturing of the symbiotic A-B pseudo-unity, so that A for the first time has to see himself as a separate person in the world, standing alone facing his future, having to make his own choices from the new position of unwanted freedom. Now he will be responsible for his relationships, unless he can rapidly enough re-invent the symbiosis with B, or with someone else pretending that nothing has happened. Similarly, of course, B has to face her separateness, but has a readier source of comfort available. Her "relationship" with C has a certain cachet of normality—it may look like a good healthy two-person relationship rather than the suicide of a symbiosis. Also, B and C are free to give up their freedom in the interest of the security of a B-C pseudo-unity.

From my experience of people living closely together, under the same roof or in a more diffused network arrangement, I would say that when jealousy (in any form) arises, there has to be at least one person strong or "wise" enough first to catalyze the emergence of a greater degree of emotional reality between the people concerned, and second, to guarantee the survival and further development of the personal wholeness of each. This latter quality is something like this: the person is acquainted, through the travail and gradually acquired discipline of his life, with the family he has internalized, carries around in his mind, repeatedly externalizes onto any other microsocial situation, and then "takes back"—cleanly enough to leave the others untransmuted by his transient alteration of their reality. Then, because he is familiar enough with this operation in his own experience, he can see through similar processes in others, so that he can function all the time in such a manner that the shifting system of internal family and actual outside presences becomes, if not clear, at least less confusing to everyone. This does not mean that the person has to become a therapist to the group and spell out interpretatively the movements from inner to outer reality and back, with the concurrent falsifications that work in both directions.

What is imperative, however, is that the persons involved should sense that at least this one person senses the interplay of reality with its derealization and then rerealization; then others might too. It is not a matter, primarily, of knowing exactly what is going on in the group, but of knowing that someone knows and because one knows of the knowing, one knows that one might know oneself. The ideal end point here, of course, is that everyone knows enough to take the load of understanding off the back of the original "knower" in the group—however great his "passion to understand men" (Sartre) might be. The knower, in fact, may have to know enough to be kind enough to himself to stop knowing and give others a chance![13]

One word that might help us to further this sense of knowing about being known is the word "witnessing." It is very much a matter of seeing what is going on between oneself and the people closest to oneself and anyone that any one of them might be in relationship with. In the jargon, this may seem like a particularly masochistic response to one's paranoia, pushing one's paranoia to the limit and almost dying or being driven mad by the persecution. Seeing may be quite literal, or it may be simply knowing what is going on, understanding it and not being in the dark.

When marriages "break up," I still feel a vestigial sense of amazement about the way that a state of not knowing about some affair that the other partner once had and now "confesses" to is contorted into an issue of jealousy and anger. In fact, if one traces back the history of the relationship, the point of the partner having the affair that the other did not "know about" was often a point of liberation in sexual and relationship terms for the other (the "betrayed" one). But the divorce carries on, of course, because there is false resentment instead of real gratitude. *But then the only evil of divorce is the prior evil of marriage.*

13 I am talking here of a person who is antithetic to the paternalistic figure, a person who is blessed with the power of uniting people to work on their relationships without interfering with these relationships, who simply catalyzes the relationship work. In fact, a leader who, while remaining a definite presence, makes everyond else a leader too. This is the *charismatic leader.* Not the leader who is pushed into power like Hitler, Churchill or Kennedy, or who voraciously seeks power like Nixon or Stalin, but the leader who, by the quality of his being, would make all people leaders. It is the necessary presence of this sort of leader that avoids replication of the family pattern in any human institution. The charismatic leader is the anti-leader, in the sense that he leads everyone into leadership.

At this point I think one has to make a distinction between generations and their possibilities. I think that if we now, always in a first-world context, take the generation of people in early middle age, and also that of people now in their mid-teens to mid-twenties (the generation gap between these two groups now seems to be little more than twelve years) we find a common problem, albeit a problem that some of us might be grateful to have: the need for a strong, central two-person relationship that is inevitably felt by others to be somewhat excluding. Whether this need will apply, in the future, to the generation still in primary school is another matter, since the rate of breakdown of the institutional fabric of bourgeois society may be rapid enough in the next decade to introduce, for them, the possibility of a less centric system of relationships. There may be a shifting system of dyads leading to a polycentric relationship structure, even though there will probably be a degree of hierarchization in the emotional significance of the various two-person relationships that each person has.

But for the present let us try to be clearer about the "strong, central, two-person relationship." As I see it, this relationship in no sense entails the formation of a closed family system, i.e., an exclusion, by relationship, of other significant relationships for each of the two people and the closely related claustration of the children within the small system of "primary" relationships. The clear possibility, now actualized by many people, is that more or less peripheral relationships with others may feed into the central two-person relationship in a way that enriches its quality on every level and reinforces its intensities. This realization, however, can again lead into euphoric idealism unless one recognizes certain qualifications. At certain stages of a two-person relationship, either or both partners may need to make certain promises. In the exploration of the relationship one may need the other person to agree not to enter into another relationship until there is full concurrence about the "right time." No-one, of course, is compelled to make or keep such a promise—the right to say "no" is fundamental. On the other hand, given the predatory nature of our society and the fact that we all internalize its predatoriness and reproduce it in our acts despite our best intentions, and in all our relationships, it seems reasonable for two people to arrive at a temporary contractual restriction on the extent of other relationships. This contract is antithetic to the marriage contract on the most essential point, the point of *relationship time.*

The marriage contract involves submission of personal need to an externally imposed time scheme. Through this submission, one's social time and space is displaced into a region of otherness, leaving an emptiness in us that "given time" (which finally takes our time away), is no longer noticed any more. If we do notice it we may want our time back, but we then find that to get our time back involves a devastating shattering of our laboriously erected security structures and the full unleashing of the archaically implanted guilt about what we are doing to the security of others. We may well give up in despair, but if we are alert enough to the issues, we find ourselves impaled on the other horn of the guilt dilemma because there is then the progressive dissemination of our despair into all the others we relate to closely and would love.

The way out of the situation seems to me to be the dawning realization that perhaps the most liberating thing we can do for other people is to do the thing that is most liberating for oneself. The most liberating thing is always the most joyful, but we must understand joy here as clearly distinct from happiness (which always devolves onto security in some form, that is to say, a deceptively comfortable restriction of one's possibilities). Joy comprehends despair, running through an end point of pain into joy again. Whereas happiness is a unitary feeling tone issuing from security, joy is the full, simultaneous expression of a spectrum: joy at one end, despair in the middle, and then joy again at the other end. It is rare enough in this culture, in my experience, for people to weep freely enough in despair. It is far rarer for a noncontradictory joy to be present through such weeping. The fact that liberation is immediately pain, and always means hard work on oneself from the decisive moment onwards, is no enigmatic irony but an issue of our internalization of an objective contradiction in bourgeois society.

In a two-person relationship that chooses its own self-evolving definition rather than a static, externally imposed definition, there is at least the chance of a respect for the natural history of a fully lived-out relationship. For instance, in any two-person relationship there is a natural fluctuation in the intensity of sexual involvement. There may be fairly long periods of mutual or one-sided sexual withdrawal which cannot be reduced to resolvable "neurotic conflict"—try as one may, and however dutifully and obediently one tries to produce sexuality. Sexual involvement with people outside the dyad can clearly break down the intradyadic withdrawal, if one most central illusion can be destroyed—*the illusion of the quantifiability of love.*

Love, of course, like every experience we may achieve, can be reduced to a state of being that may be reduced in turn to the status of a commodity and then fetishized like any other commodity. It becomes a sort of parcel, with socially prescribed dimensions that cannot be exceeded in the circumstances of any specific relationship. One has (one is led to believe and then further leads oneself to believe) only so much love to offer. If one gives almost all one's love to one other person, one has proportionately very little to parcel out to others. If one operates with this naive algebra, a corollary must be that any act of loving is experienced as loss of a certain inner quantity of love. Now it seems to me that the illusory character of this postal-package theory of love derives from an oversimplification in understanding the full structure of the act of loving. This act subsumes the following experiential moments, if we take the case of person A loving person B: A internalizes a more or less "whole picture" of B over a certain period of time; the time, in clock terms, may be years or seconds —the latter, because loving need not imply long-term formation or long-term commitment to this particular two-person relationship which would involve many considerations above the base line of love.

"During" and "after"[14] this act of internalization another form of action takes place, and this is an action on the internalizing act. This second act, if it is to demystify a love possibility, strikes away as many as possible of the previous internalizations one has made of others in one's life and leaves a relatively unaltered presence in person A's experience of person B. These prior internalizations cling to any new internalization and thus would transform B's potential presence in A's experience into a relative absence. If, say, A identifies B very closely with his mother on some level that he is hardly aware of, he cannot, precisely to that extent, love B insofar as B—as B—is rendered absent by the identification, and one can only love on the basis of internal presence (although one can certainly be happy enough with an absence).

14 We have now left the region of object chronology and "before" and "after" refer to subjective time or one's "temporalization" or self-timing of oneself.

Next, A registers, in the experience of B, his (A's) registration of the presence of B. The communication may be in words or may be extraverbal, or both. In any case, because of a further action on A's part, B recognizes her recognition by A; and recognizes her recognition of his (A's) recognition of her.

The next level of the structure, which is of particular significance, is an action on B's part which lets A see that B recognizes his recognition by A. The significance here is that what we have termed A's act of loving depends for its very existence on an action, perhaps subtle, hardly obvious, on B's part. In ordinary social relating B may suppress her act of expressing registration of A's registration of her, just as A may suppress his awareness of B's suppression. This becomes a heightened difficulty in relationships called psychotherapeutic, where A (in this case the "therapist") must refuse the suppression of his awareness of B's suppression of her, so that a healing love becomes possible, that is to say, a love that is disciplined enough to avoid falling into a false commitment that violates the respect that each must have for the time of the other if a fatal (but once again comfortable enough) engulfment is to be avoided.

But let us go back to the beginning of all this, because so far we have dealt with the preconditional structure of love rather than its axial definition. When I wrote of the stripping away of the clinging internal traces of other presences, what was implicit in this was the elimination of alien elements that might contaminate the new internal presence. In other words, the other (B) might be loved or hated or (more usually) both—in the guise of another. ("Another," here, we might call non-$A^1$, non-$A^2$, non-$A^n$, that is to say, one of or any of A's previous internalizations of others.) What is definitive of love is that paring away of feeling, falsely transposed onto the new presence, which leaves one free to love—and the mutually recognized freedom to love *is* love. Of course if A becomes free to love B, he may well hate B if B gives him reason to do so, but an inspired guess here might be that, if transposed negative feeling is relegated thoroughly enough, the only new resentment would be based on a violation of the love discipline, which is the failure to alertly respect the internal time needs of the other. The words, "Give me time," so often uttered in relationships, may be understood, not as a request *for* love, consideration and patience, but as a pained, confused enunciation of the wish *to* love. But then, in a world where time is tensioned into clock springs and is symbolized by a murky social praxis out of all reality and into money, shit, schedules and ritualized anti-work, who can wait any longer?

An experience developed in London over the last decade has centered on the development of dehierarchizing communities[15] in which some of the members have been, or in other cases would have been, psychiatrically stigmatized as being "mad" or some jargon equivalent, such as "schizophrenic." It seems to me relevant to consider these communities here because, apart from their intrinsic qualities of radical innovation, their implications extend far beyond the narrow confines of psychiatry and "revolutions" in psychiatry and demand a historical reevaluation of all human acts that have been regarded as mad—ultimately demanding, I believe, the integration of "the mad experience" in the minds of each of us, where it will represent an extension of awareness rather than be a source of frightened victimization of a minority. Also, with

15 Communities founded under the auspices of the Philadelphia Association, London. The principal one of these communities has been Kingsley Hall, in East London.

more immediate practical import, one inevitably finds that when people group together to form liberatory communes and networks without explicit psychiatric reference, similar problems arise in relation to dealing with disturbance in some of the members, with temptations in the others to deal with such disturbance by a violence that would reduplicate that of the whole society, that is, by operations of excluding and shutting up the disturbed person.

Since the communities to which I have referred have been described in a number of publications, I shall simply list certain principles of their organization, or rather anti-organization.

Firstly, there is no psychiatric diagnosis, and therefore the first step in the invalidation of persons is not taken. The actual meaning of "diagnosis," in socially effective terms, is running a sword through the heart of gnosis. It is the murder of the possibility of knowing the other person, effected by displacement of the reality of the person into the limbo of social pseudo-objectivity. To label someone as a "schizophrenic," "paranoid," a "psychopath," some sort of "sexual pervert," an "addict," an "alcoholic," is to direct one's missile-bearing rockets against a certain city. After a while, and after a bit of forgetting, pressing the button becomes so indifferent a matter that it is a nonact. The bomb is action, acting on itself to negate itself. Then, although its source has been actively lost, we end up with a real devastation of minds and bodies.

The fact that no resort is made to false categorization of persons in these communities is preconditioned by the dehierarchization of the group. There is either a progressive or an immediate breakdown of the binary role structure of doctor or nurse *versus* patient. Some of the people, if they were transposed to the institutional structure of a mental hospital, would be called psychiatrists, others would be called patients. In the communities, however, there are simply people, some of whom are more in touch than others with the changing reality of the group and the changes developing within each person in the group, but the people with this charisma of knowing might well be the "patients" in the conventional setting. In short, the communities are places for people to *be,* and not places to *be treated.* Being is active and alive, it is opting out of the false passivity of being treated or, in any sense, being dealt with by others.

The positive center of the experience of the community, however, resides in the guarantee that some other person will always accompany one on one's journey into and through one's self. This "guarantee," to turn bourgeois language against itself, implies not a big corporation with assets duly listed in the financial section of *The Times* but an implicit promise made by one or several people to other people. One needs, if one is to go deeply enough through experiences of personal disintegration and then reintegration, of the destructuring of one's life pattern and then the restructuring of it, the promise that someone else neutrally enough—that is, sufficiently without a personal axe to grind—will be with one attentively throughout the experience. What is required is a noninterfering person who is quite simply a person who does not compulsively have to interfere. Someone who will let the other be.[16]

Beyond this, the antipsychiatry community follows the principles of any other commune. For instance, the dialectic between solitude and being with other people that

16 This applies to other areas of medicine beyond psychiatry. For instance, how many gynecologists can allow their patients to have their own babies, i.e., the patient's babies, not the gynecologist's? I would suggest, as part of the gynecologist's training course, the procedure of sitting for at least one hour a week listening to one of his patients talking about being a woman and having a baby.

achieves its own synthesis in the activity of coming and going—a synthesis that might be imaginatively reproduced by the image of a person, at Wimbledon with a television box, who does not any longer turn his head to right and then left, but looks straight ahead at the box because that is where the game is after all.

This dialectic is reflected in the architecture of the center, and devolves onto the principle of single cells (which, of course, other people can move into and share with the room inhabitant by free and fully acknowledged choice between him and them) and a common living area that anyone can spend more or less time in. If one person so elects they need see no-one else for weeks, months or years. When one wants or needs other people, one knows the places to find them. Simple cooking arrangements in each room (or at least two kitchens for a group of twenty people) would make it unnecessary for people to argue about the use of a central kitchen, which is always one of the principal territorial-imperative stumbling-blocks in a commune.

Another, related, principle that applies to any other commune is the respect of the right for anyone to say "*no*" to the demands or wishes of any other. The "no" may be temporary or permanent, but in any case demands full attentiveness because any violation of the "no" means a violation of one's own time needs, if we consider these as a synthesis of outer (social, biological) time and inner time, and also, on a third level, the time one needs to take to effect this synthesis.

Next, there is the principle of knowing that someone knows. The expression of this principle might take several forms. One form is the experience of meeting one's family with the presence of a mediator, so that for the first time one may see one's family objectively as the quasi-totality it has made itself for one, dominating one's life from the inside of one's mind and reinforcing its internal presence by a multitude of external maneuvers, binds, traps and so on that are so elusive that one feels one must be suffering from paranoid delusions. One experienced other person, however, in the course of perhaps only one hour's meeting, may help one get one's family out of one's head and into a field of full vision. If one's mother is the person who knows one "inside out," what does one make of a situation in which one knows that someone else, outside the family structure, knows one's mother's knowing oneself inside out from the inside out? If, as the child of one's parents, one knows that the knower too can be known, the commune might even offer a liberatory hope to parents, and beyond parents, to psychiatrists.

On the basis of experience of communities of this sort, one begins to ask questions that get as apparently nonsensical as this: What is the difference between the mental hospital and the university, why cannot universities become mental hospitals, and why cannot mental hospitals become universities? The exterior design is similar enough, the administration block and various departments, villas, laboratories, occupational therapy and so on. Some universities have fences and guards' lodges to check on who is coming or going. The irony in this is that probably no-one ever goes, and certainly no-one ever comes. Both institutions are rife with phony concern of a confused, paternalistic-maternalistic sort on the part of the "guardians" that operates against the "guarded." Both are fair mothers (the alma mater) with breasts full of the old poison, tranquilizers in every conceivable form, everything from the right pill for the right patient to the right job for the right graduate. Both are terrified of sexuality and, for that matter, of the reality of human relationships in any form. Both institutions are run by the sad, grey, anonymous petty timeservers of a timeserving society that can only internally justify its own servitude by the enslavement of others, who might run the thing much better themselves precisely insofar as they are less frightened and no longer need the old sterile security structures of those who pretend to be their mentors.

Considerations of this sort lead us on to another sort of community that one might, archaically enough, call the spiritual, the esoteric, the gnostic. Defining the new meaning of revolution in the first world today, I think one has now to envisage a full incorporation into the mass social movement not only of forms of activity that are personally liberating in the sense of "therapy" but also of activities that are "spiritual" in a certain sense. The sense I mean is radical dissolution of false egoic structures that one is brought up to experience oneself in. The dissolution of a brainwashed self-image that one is viciously indoctrinated into by the kindest, closest, best-intentioned people in the world—one's parents and one's teachers. One thing, for sure, is that one can show no generosity or compassion to them until one can let them see that one will no longer submit to the throttling grip of the rope that is around *their* necks. The only way to compassionate involvement with others is the short cut of one's own liberation.

In this sense I would envisage one aspect of revolution as the universal unleashing of a full spirituality, in which forms of religious experience, in any and every spiritual tradition, go back beyond the point in their history where they became institutionalized, bureaucratized and depersonalized, and become personally relevant on the face-to-face confrontation group of the commune, where no-one proselytizes anyone but himself. It's a matter of realizing that there *is* nothing to join beyond a point of self-juncture

—more brutally, it is a matter of meeting oneself and then deciding whether or not one wants to continue the relationship.

Of the many forgotten possibilities that we have to repossibilize, the two foremost seem to me to be the possibilities of remembering one's dreams (reassembling the torn-apart structures that we produce as the dream anatomist secreted as such from ourselves) and fully experiencing the range of possibilities of killing oneself. The right dream is a remembered and recognized dream. The right suicide is precisely the precise one one does not commit. The most authentic suicide in our age (that is, after Christ's) is probably Kirilov's in *The Possessed* by Dostoevsky, and that, of necessity, was fictional.

Two of the main functions of the commune must be, firstly, to reinvent the possibility of registering one's dreams with oneself and then with at least one other person, preferably the person one sleeps with; and secondly, to recover the lost adolescent fantasies of suicide and an even more lost infantile vision of death, and to talk freely to other people about these fantasies.

At the beginning of this chapter I wrote of the need to reconsider, in the most basic terms, the meaning of revolution in first-world countries. It seems to me that this reconsideration must issue from microsocial experience, worked out in face-to-face confrontation groups. If we are to talk of urban guerrilla warfare as the decisive strategy in first-world countries, we have to recognize a multiplicity in the weaponry that people might use. Molotov cocktails certainly have their place in a significantly organized, student-worker rebellion, in organized anti-crime, such as looting shops, and in burning antipopular institutions, which is obviously dictated by the objective context of a black ghetto rebellion. But there are other sorts of bombs to use, too. For me, it is a revolutionary act if in the course of months or years a person transcends the major bits of his micro- and macrosocial conditioning in the direction of the spontaneous self-assertion of full personal autonomy, which *in itself* is a decisive act of counterviolence against the system. It means that the person is *ready*, in a way that few are. Beyond the one-person scale, but always coming in a sense from "one person," there is the explosive potential of a group or network who, in the course of a long travail, demonstrate the possibility of firstly viable and secondly good developing relationships that are antithetic along the most essential parameters to bourgeois relationships, which are imposed, unchosen, uncreative and uncreating, and which are always on the model of the nuclear family, in either its original or its replicated forms.

In an earlier essay[17] I wrote of the need to develop Revolutionary Centers of Consciousness. These would take the form of anti-institutional, spontaneous groupings of people who operate outside the formal bureaucratic structures of their factory, school, university, hospital, broadcasting corporation, art institution (in the sense of either art school or gallery politics) and so on. In this form of grouping there would be no suppression of the personal reality of any member in the mode of serialization (i.e., forming bus queues of people working in the institutional structure, waiting for a bus that never arrives). Also, there would be a paradigmatic influence mushrooming out to other potential groups.

The revolutionary nature of these groups (which, without a program, are already emerging anyhow) lies in the exploding of the contradiction between the desperately controlling operations of bourgeois society that would

17 D. G. Cooper, "Beyond Words," in D. G. Cooper, ed., *The Dialectics of Liberation* (Harmondsworth, Middlesex: Penguin, 1968).

anonymize, order and categorize people, and the impulse actually *in* people, despite this, to shout out their names in the world and to announce their work to the world—in fact, to show themselves to the world because they can begin to look at their selves themselves.

But things cannot rest at this level of rapidly spreading subversion from the micropolitical base of personal liberation. The fulfillment of liberation comes only with effective macropolitical action. So the Centers of Revolutionary Consciousness have also to become Red Bases.[18] Macropolitical action here must be essentially negative, and takes the form of rendering bourgeois power structures impotent by any and every means. The means might be a *revolutionary mimesis* of the tactics of the bourgeois power structure. The structure is greedy, it devours people and consumes their work, shitting out the indigestible residue as pay, as obscene holiday camps and so on. So why not mimic the greed of the system by following its example as closely as possible? After all, one could hardly be more moral than that. In other words, if bosses or university authorities make concessions, one demands and exacts more and more "concessions" until *they* realize that they had nothing to give in the first place. Then, having abolished that false family structure, all one has to do is to make sure it is not set up again. Revolution becomes, not an historical act, but history itself—continuous Revolution. Or again, one may show that bourgeois power structures are powerless, apart from the power that we obediently invest them with, by arranging their disorganization. A few very simple but carefully concerted actions might do this.

Beyond this there are the more conventional tactics of

18 I see this happening most effectively in the formation of street communes, where people with good relationships and a similar political orientation buy flats and houses in the same street and engage in sharing at every level.

strike and sit-in, but work on the micropolitical level can rid these tactics of their economism, that is to say, that in a first-world context it can never be simply a matter of more bread, but more bread and much more reality. What we want, in short, is not to chew our loaf but to consume the system, so that at last we might get a taste of ourselves.

# The End of Education— A Beginning

We have not learned anything,
we don't know anything,
we don't understand anything,
we don't sell anything,
we don't help,
we don't betray,
and
we will not forget.

—Czech Freedom Poster

FIRST, one has to clear the field of discourse of certain presuppositions as to what education is about. So one draws one's pen through notions such as graded examinations, divisions between infants' and primary and secondary schools, and ultimately, any segregation of ages and sexes, examination-determined durations of various university courses, the Ph.D., transition rites from one absurd limbo to another limbo that the candidate is expected to be concerned about as a real end, and so on. The validation of the act of drawing one's pen through these frenetic surface rituals (that shy off from the realities of initiation in the direction of a simple-minded indoctrination into a conformism that confuses people to an extent where their critical awareness of the situation hardly operates any longer) is ready at hand. I shall try to make this clear, although many others are beginning to do so now.

I think we have to define education very widely indeed, because anything short of this requisite width would have the effect of a cord around the neck of a strangled victim.

So let us take education as the self-totalizing movement of interplay between the peson's unending formation of his self and the formative influences from other people acting on him throughout his life. "Formation" here means the emergence of a certain *kind* of person that subsumes specialized areas of expertise. It means transcendence of the subject/object split, insofar as the person, and *ultimately* he alone, synthesizes these poles and becomes the active user of the passive moment of his experience and the passive witness of his activity and that of the others to a point where the witnessing itself becomes an act, and so on. Further, the phrase "throughout his life" does not refer to a person's biological life span, countable in years. It does not exclude the fact that we may, in some discernible sense, live and experience before and after the biological facts of birth and death, nor does it exclude the further possibility of a concrete phenomenology[19] of such experience.

Let us consider how a certain form of life is planned for us (we, of course, being planners in turn for the lives of

19 By "phenomenology," I mean here the direct experience of a person or object without the intervention of preconceptions about that person or object. It is a matter of apprehending the person or object in its pristine reality rather than through the obscuring panes of glass that represent our preconcepts.

others) from way beyond our biological beginnings as well as those of our parents and their parents—we shall leave in parentheses for the moment the extension of these plans into the region of our corporeal death.

Research into the genesis of schizophrenia in families, carried out in the last two decades, has shown clearly enough how madness becomes intelligible if one understands the systems of communication-action that go on in a nuclear family. The more recent developments in these studies show how important it is to include the *third generation* back, the parents of the parents of the person said to be mad, if one is adequately to extend this intelligibility. I would say that not only does one have to include the fourth generation back in this sort of study but that, to achieve a full intelligibility, one has to plunge into a past that goes beyond the conscious recall of any family member the person has ever known. This remoter past is recaptured in dreams, in "psychotic experience" and certain drug-induced states, but I believe also in a suitably structured present, experiential situation that must become very centrally the concern of education. This is so because what I have said about the understanding of someone called schizophrenic applies to the comprehension of the life of any person, once the deceptive stain of normality is flushed away.

To illustrate this point, I shall quote a critical dream that was dreamed recently by a young man who directed films, aged thirty-one, Jewish. He had left home at the age of twenty-three, he thought in fairly decisive terms, and had married a girl from a notoriously anti-Semitic country. They were at a crisis in their relationship, and after having gone through a number of family sessions (in relation to a younger sister who had had a "schizophrenic" breakdown) and several individual sessions (in relation to his "marital crisis" and a "work inhibition"), he had the following dream:

The dream he dreamt seemed to belong to everyone in the world. It seemed to have been addressed through him to masses of unknown but very definite people. A phrase that recurred throughout the dream was "I've lost the book." In the dream he went to a house, an Arab village in the Middle East. After a dream interlude in which he related to a white and to a black girl, he emerged from the top of the house onto a desert landscape, where he came upon a hut where he met an ancient rabbi. He sat on a stool, a very small one, before the rabbi. All the persecutory feeling of the earlier part of the dream seemed to evaporate, and he was filled with feelings of loss and sadness. Then, all of a sudden, he burst into laughter and fell off the stool. There was a momentary slapstick interlude with the sage in which they both laughed their heads off. He awoke with a very powerful feeling that "it wasn't just *my* dream." In a sense, the young man had followed his umbilical cord to its proper place of attachment and then, in the explosion of laughter between the two people, the cord was broken, leaving him separate in the world, seeing the other as an other.

There is, I believe, quite a case to be made out for the fact that the intra-uterine period (let alone what happens before that) represents, not seven tenths or eight tenths of the iceberg, but maybe, to make a suitable joke of numbers, even nine tenths of the experience that any person ever has. A level of intra-uterine experience extends throughout our lives; it is certainly not limited to the original nine months. How can we remember, precisely because of the prior question, which is how could we forget, the cascade of blood in our mother's abdominal aorta, with its regular, disciplined, biological clockwork echoing fractionally a more distant heartbeat, contradicted by her far more spontaneous, nervous and calm borborygmi, the incredible orchestration of breath sounds, the felt creak of muscle tensions and relaxations, her hand that feels our movements and the careful careless palpation of the doctor's hand and the midwife's. The drugs to keep us going and those that were intended to get rid of us. The fantasies our mother had because of the fantasies that others from infinitely back in history had about her. The curling over of our neural cord and the memory of the genetic possibility of omitting its completion. The formation of our sex that challenges all our subsequent freedom to modify it from time to time. Then the experience of coming into the world of garish, clinical light into dutiful, undelighted hands, the clanging of chromium instruments and aseptic trays, the importunate imperative between the fingers of the midwife's hands that tells us to wait, maybe even go back a while until "they" are ready, disguised as the moment of *our* readiness to emerge into the world. And then, almost orgasmically, we come and are laid on the platter, to be consumed in an ultimate infanticide by the world of devoured, bone-picked, skeletal people. Then we howl and, incidentally, inflate our solid lungs, but the howl is remembered as something we will never do again—unless it's in a car with the windows rolled up, driving along a motorway at eighty miles an hour. *Bodily* felt and acted protest ends there—but there may be other forms of protest against the innate and natally destroyed right to scream "No" to the world. No, let us start again, better this time, because this time will be our time. The doctors and the mothers will have to attend to our time and find theirs through ours, because the alternative is Beckett's image of the gravedigger-accoucheur—who waits in the grave he has just dug to catch the infant as dropped from just over the grave from our mother's womb into his hands—which are her hands and our hands.

We are in fact dealing here with a critical phase of education, but education in a bivalent sense. It is education for the emerging person, interacting with education for the mother and the doctor and midwife. Education for the adults means, most immediately, being open to the experience of the infant in the sense of allowing experiential resonances to reach down to their own birth experiences, which I believe are more *taught out* of them by a highly conscious, miseducational process than repressed in the familiar psychoanalytic sense. Repression is a highly specific, well-defined term in original Freudian theory and certainly operates significantly as a prereflective teaching from mother to child in the first year or two of life, as well as later. That is to say, the child internalizes aspects of the mother's presence that exclude the holding of the birth experience, but the mother has been subject, not only to a similar situation with her mother, but to a host of conscious and consciously applied social experiences that make her make the infant *forget.* The evident reason for this is that the most tabooed areas of human experience are those involving birth and death—let alone prebirth and postdeath experience. The delineation of the operation of incest taboos and sexual taboos more generally was a necessary historical introduction to these more extensive machinations of the man who always puts his terror into the word "No."

So we see what in effect is an encirclement of repression by a multiplicity of conscious maneuvers that can be pinned down fairly concretely and attached by a countereducation. The little girl, before she can be *her own* baby, is plied with object-babies (the more "perfect" dolls being the most expensive) so that she can learn to forget her experience of birth and childhood and become, not her own child, but simply childlike or, if later in life she wants to return to this area, childish (regressive, hysteric, etc.). So she is educated to be a mother like her mother and like all other mothers who were educated, not to be themselves, but to be "like mothers." I am reminded of a story told me by a colleague of a young man in the United States (subsequently, of course, diagnosed psychotic) who, with a time bomb, blew up a fully laden passenger plane carrying his mother off on holiday. Prior to this, he had sent his mother a Mother's Day card inscribed, "To someone who has been just like a mother to me." Well, perhaps that time bomb is under each of our seats at this moment, because we are confused about who is innocent and who is guilty and we are confused because our blocking compulsion is that we have to ask the question. On this level, how different is any of our fates from that of the hunted guerrilla fighter in Vietnam or Angola or Brazil who grips his gun and says, in his own most appropriate metaphor, "I am here, I am myself, let me be and let me choose those I want to be with, because if you don't . . ."

The movement from repression (which can be modified and socially adapted but essentially remains with us to be used, if possible, for the social good) to straightforward suppression is very clear today. The suppression may be devious and may possess a certain cunning in the guise of liberal sophistication, but in real terms it comes to arming oneself with all the weapons available. *Paranoia as resolvable fantasy has had its day. Persecution, a real social fact, now holds the field.* If we have residual paranoid fantasies and superego problems, perhaps *the act of resolution is to use them.* If we are concerned enough, we may wish that psychoanalysis, one of the potentially greatest liberatory instruments we have, avoid reactionary misuse. If we are less concerned about this, we may simply wish to eliminate the *ground* of political reaction, which is assiduously taught nonexperience.

All this relates very closely to the situation of young people battling to free themselves into their own futures, as distinct from futures vicariously and lovingly prescribed for them by parents and teachers (who can never form associations for their own salvation without the overriding confusion of that pretext "for the children"). The false project here, patently, is to seek liberation by altering one's parents—*one* will be free at last if *they* are free at last. This is the issue of parents' use of "their" children to be their parents, to absorb their aggression (as in overt punishment of the children to get one's "own" back on, or own self back from, one's own parents, or in more subtle deformations of their aspiring, autonomous projects). The bourgeois nuclear family apparently cannot function without this role reversal that confirms the prior role system. A reversed reversal, whereby the child has to keep the family together at all costs or—in terms of the usual verification—at the cost of the most expensive tranquilizer on the National Health Service prescription list. So once again, it's a matter of how to write through the prescription that would proscribe us.

If one cannot alter one's parents, if one reaches a point of generosity where one can allow them to have their own problems at last, one can at least consider altering one's teachers. This might involve the "dangerous" transition of a primary school teacher from being a substitute parent to being a person. If the primary school teacher is the first "significant other" outside the family, as he—or, more usually, she—often is, how can he clarify his "being outside," without invoking censure or dismissal from the petty officialdom of local education authorities? Similarly, how can lecturers in universities and colleges avoid a similar fate? The answer, not an easy one, is doubtless to maximize one's clarity within the system, to become as clear as possible about what one wants to learn (not teach, since teaching is pure collaboration) and then to aim at as massive a drop-out of teachers and pupils and students as possible to the point of stopping, in concert with similar movements in other institutions, the operations of one's particular school or college as finally and as decisively as possible, and then, circumadventing all plots to reintroduce one into the system by ghettoization or any other means.[20]

Then it is a question of where one drops out into.

What I am proposing is a totally dehierarchized, mobile structure that is in continuous revolution, and therefore can generate further revolution beyond the limits of its structure. The university (or, at this stage of history, what has to be called the anti-university, counter-university, free university or some such term[21]) is a fairly extended network of people, anything in present terms from fifty or sixty to two to three hundred people. In the case of the larger number, the group-unifying principle is that anyone can present an extended account of their work experience (which includes, needless to say, experience of anyone else in the network or the network itself or any segment of the

20 Since the May Rebellion of 1968 in France, the authorities have followed a policy of gathering radical thinkers together in one place, to facilitate the suppression of new thought. A blatant example is the expulsion of Jacques Lacan, on an absurd pretext, from the École Normale Supérieure, and the subsequent invitation for him to teach at Vincennes on the outskirts of Paris.

21 I am referring here not only to spontaneous free universities generated by rebellion within existing universities but to other prototype experiences, some of them very different from what I describe in this chapter, such as the New Experimental College in Denmark, the Free University of New York, and the anti-university of London (sponsored by the Institute of Phenomenological Studies—a "shadow" anti-organization which also "organized" the Congress on the Dialectics of Liberation in London—see *The Dialectics of Liberation*, edited by David Cooper (Harmondsworth, Middlesex: Penguin, 1968)—and disappears to reappear if and when it chooses).

network) to anyone else who chooses to listen, by simple arrangement—for which one takes the initiative oneself. Inevitably, certain charismatic leaders or teachers attract groups to them, but the definitive nature of the charismatic leader, in this context, is that he does not appropriate the charisma of others, so that groups disengage from the initiatory group, taking with them their own charismatic centers that are similarly dispensed and extended in a manner that allows a free relating back to the group source of the group—or not, if such reference is not required. In any case, there is a decisive breakdown of the academic, bureaucratic opposition of the teacher and the taught.

The context of the group interactions issues from a consensual affirmation of interest and concern, but consensus is disciplined by the authority demonstrated by one person or several people in each group. This is quite antithetic to authoritarianism. At certain times needs coalesce into the desire for the rigorous and scholarly treatment of one issue by a particular person, or the planning of a sequence of explorations of one issue with reading planned by the person with most authority in that area. The significant point, however, is that true discipline and rigor can only be developed from a solid base of freedom and trust in the group. The "qualifications" of the person who initiates a group are in terms of his or her prior achievements in writing, talking, creative work and political work. I intend these terms in a very wide sense indeed; for example, creative work includes the poetry of gesture of a fully lived-through madness. Beyond this no qualifications are required of anyone, nor is there any age limit. Nor is there any "examination" structure or "degree." If someone requires a statement about the work he has done in the groups, this would take the form of a detailed consensus statement compiled by the group—*including* the person who wants to use such a statement. To play the system, of course, a special testimonial might be written by a "teacher" with a reputation that is recognized in the world outside. There is no way around the difficulty that people in a prerevolutionary society will have to earn money to live. People may have to do teaching jobs that get paid, or use student grants provided for official university work, or any other sort of job.

The cells would function either within an official university or school as an antidote to that system, or quite independently. In the latter case, they would function from the base of a certain factory, or as meetings arranged in private houses,[22] pubs or coffee houses, and maybe in the future churches (not only church halls) may be taken over for meetings. Finances and care of premises are the conjoint responsibility of the group.

In the former case, however, one has a chance to appropriate facilities from the appropriators of minds. University accommodation is taken over for the use of the cells, including purposes of eating, sleeping and making love. Participation by staff is obviously welcome, but no imposition of official hierarchic structure is permitted. Free access to any group includes attendance by nonacademic staff and anyone from outside the university. People from outside the university will naturally be invited to give sustained presentations of their work.

If it is objected that technical learning, say in the sciences and medicine, may be rendered impossible by this "anarchic" development, it should be clear that the groups I have described are a human complement to *technē.* Of course technical learning goes on, but it is no longer *merely*

22 For instance, in the anti-university group that I have attended over the last two years, each meeting is arranged *ad hoc* in a private house or flat, and the locale tends to be fixed by word-of-mouth network contact, so that one may not know it until the day of the meeting.

that and certainly moves from the situation of mass lectures—which are or could be duplicated and distributed, anyhow, as extensions to textbooks—into face-to-face seminar groups in which a full "apprenticeship" is lived out in the contact of minds. Again, however, written examinations, answers to questions, will be ended. Assessments must be made *in work* and self-presentation, and not in some ludicrous and irrelevant anxiety kitchen.

One of the main functions of the cells (which macropolitically are Red Bases) is to transcend the difference between therapy and learning; inevitably, one of the obstacles is the strong impulse to limit the group activity to therapy in the conventional sense. This reflects the difference between group leaders, who in practice have tended to be either teachers or therapists. Teachers often feel uncertain about dealing with the group impulse towards therapy; therapists are similarly in difficulty about articulating their experience into sustained, general enough statement. Perhaps the answer, however, is not for teachers and therapists to get into their own groups to learn to overcome these differences of background, but to be taught and "therapeutized" by others in the group who seem able to do this. Of course they may have to wait. Or there may be a compromise in which several teachers and therapists get together to look at their problems ruthlessly and with no critical holds barred, in a group which would be open to any other members of their various cells who cared to come and comment on their comments about each other's work.

There is a hunger, now quite universal in the first world, for supreme teachers, spiritual masters who will, if they do not solve all one's problems, at least point out the right way to the right end. One of the most marked characteristics of cultural imperialism is not the imposition of first-world cultural patterns on the third world, which is violent enough, but the parasitic sucking of wisdom in any form from older civilizations. The results of this amount to a reactionary mystification that knows nothing of mysticism. If, say, some elements of Mahayana Buddhism are transferred to the West without regard to critical differences in social reality between Bhutan and San Francisco, a quietism is generated that colludes fully with the exploitative system. True mystics have always been intensely aware of the nature of the circumambient society and, in this sense, have been truly political men.

All the same, when we talk of a revolutionary university and a renewed sense of learning that takes in every level of human experience, that breaks out of[23] the confines of the buildings and curricula of schools and universities, we have, I believe, to redefine the meaning of "teacher" so that it takes in functions and ways of being that come from other places on earth and other ages. For instance, the true function of a teacher comes very close to the prophetic function. The prophet looks from his present through his past into all our pasts, and then into our future. He abnegates concern with his future in the interest of clarity about the future of all around him. He denies exceptionality in his vision of himself because he knows he is merely actualizing a teaching potential that resides in each of us, and he knows that sometimes this potential is especially strong in those who heed him least. Rather than present a vision to others, he points the way to a possible co-vision that arises out of meeting. When he talks to a group of people, he knows that usually there is a *meeting* between him and a

23 It is ironic that students in a recent protest at the London School of Economics, who were trying to break *out of* the institution, were compelled to break *in* through the doors to occupy the emptiness of the university with some human reality.

few others. Beyond this, there is only a foregathering of those who can only hear without listening. The prophet's plea always is: "If you listen to me, you will hear yourselves at last—then we might listen to each other, and then we might see where we are and where we are going!"

The guru who is a pseudomessiah, on the other hand—and all messiahs are pseudomessiahs—would impose his vision and would have a following rather than a meeting. He is the only one, the leader, whereas the prophetic teacher is the one who discovers his prophetic powers in others, who thus in some sense have priority. This gets close to a similar principle that operates on the political level: false leaders are simply shadowy presences, with artificial, "big man" images passively regurgitated by nonhuman, institutionalized social processes—for example, the Hitlers, Churchills, Kennedys, etc. The true leadership principle is embodied by men like Fidel Castro and Mao Tse-tung, who lead by almost refusing to be leaders, in the sense that they diffuse the quality of leadership outwards so that the minds of millions of people become enlivened with *their own* qualities of leadership and each person becomes the unique origin of struggle.

One of the main functions of the teacher, then, is to progressively break down the pervading illusion of impotence. Not only in academic institutions but in every institution in our society, people must be helped to realize how the power of the ruling élite and its bureaucracy is *nothing*, nothing but *their* refused and externalized power. Then it is a matter of recuperation of that power, and the recuperative strategy is quite simple: act against the "rules" and *the act itself converts the illusory power in them into real power in us.* It always amazes me how limited people feel significant talk to another person to be. If one states a significant insight about oneself to even one other person, or perhaps states an insight one has about them, the ramification of this statement through an indefinite number of others can be astounding—and usually, unfortunately, not recognized as what it is. One significant enough insight may radically alter relationships in that person's family and also in an extending network of people beyond that. Thus one "ordinary" person's one significant insight into a personal or wider social reality can affect hundreds of people. If the penny drops more often than once, the influence is proportionately greater. Many people who express "omnipotent delusions" about the extension of the influence of their minds over the minds of others or ideas of connection with apparently remóte people, or ideas of being influenced by others equally remote, are in fact stating their experience of what I have been describing, but in socially unaccepted terms. They then collude, on the basis of a prior conditioning to the victim status, with their invalidation by society —by, for instance, including in their network of influence institutions as absurd as Scotland Yard, the Queen of England, the President of the United States, or the B.B.C. In fact the essential aspect of what they are saying, as distinct from its surface coloration, is truer than, for instance, anything represented by the banal institutions that they obediently refer to.

One young man I knew felt his life at a certain critical time to be so devastated by the falsity around him, in terms both of his immediate relationships and less immediate social structures, that he decided to stage a one-man invasion of the B.B.C. His object was to tell the truth about the falsity that he had now recognized, and to tell it for the first time. His invasion was completely nonviolent and put into words, and he may well have told a certain truth for the first time on the B.B.C., but, of course, he was promptly whipped away by a gang of policemen and put on a course of electroconvulsive treatment at his local mental hospital. It has hitherto seemed, in our culture, to be a social impossibility for anyone without anxiety and panic responses to receive a communication that eludes the barren, evasive platitudes of normal social discourse.

# The Other Shore of Therapy

*Gate, Gate, Paragate, Parasamgate, bodhi svaha.*
(Gone, gone, gone to that other shore, safely passed to that other shore.)

—Ancient Buddhist incantation

One of the most grotesque illusions that afflicts life projects, whether these be individual, group or collective projects, is the notion of "The Perfect End." It also sounds most reasonable and creditable to form a clear idea of a life goal. Indeed, how can one not?

The notion of the end usually takes the form of a perfect, liberating relationship in which all negativity will finally be transcended in a perfect love union, or it is the perfect trip that finally gets one "there" (no questions asked about where one came from in order to get there, or where—if anywhere—"there" is), or it is the perfect orgasm that knocks one's animality and one's spirituality into one nature, or it is the perfect work project in which one really fulfills oneself—if only with the emptiness of one's self. But nowhere is the grotesquerie more apparent than in the idea of maturity, which is frequently posited as a goal of psychotherapy. In effective terms, maturity means a sellout to the dominant values of bourgeois society, achieved through a plethora of particular consciousnesses but in total unawareness of the historical significance of one's own, disowned transformation.

The only sense of the "mature man" that I find meaningful must be in these terms. First, it takes "a man" to live out the reality of the woman that he is. It takes even more of a man, "the mature man," to live out the reality of the child that he is. The mature man is the truly childlike man, since when one goes back far enough into the infantile and prebirth moments of one's history, and when one does not stop there, one discovers ultimately a wise old woman-man in one's self that is the experiential token of maturity, of a remote ripeness that may rot very fast in one's self that, if one is in time (that is, timely rather than immured in time), is only but not quite on the point of going bad. In any case, there has to be a significant divergence from the ordinary use of words like "man," "woman," "child," "maturity," "aging," and beyond these words, constructs like "father," "mother," "one's own children," "brother," "sister" and the rest of it.

If maturity has to be swiveled the right way up, so that it under-stands rather than stands on its head, there has to be a reciprocal revision of its apparent antithesis, neurosis. To commence the unuse of the word "neurosis," let us regard it as a way of being that is made to seem childish by one's fear of the fear of others about one's becoming childlike. Bourgeois society bars Dostoevskian idiots with no praise at all. At least by being stigmatized "neurotic" one is precipitated into a real region of social fear for which one might, without perverseness, be truly grateful. The fear is the fear of madness, of being childlike or even being before-one's-origins, so that any act may cohere others against oneself to suppress any spontaneous gesture that has socially disruptive, archaic resonances. "In" "neurosis," one lends false primacy to the reactions of others and then collusively and obligingly invites their fear into oneself. Neurosis, then, is a complex strategy (that inevitably gets arrested) of fighting one's way back into one's own head, first, and then back into one's body, "and then" . . .

Neurosis, at least, is in the right direction—not something going wrong—and therapy, in the best sense, is concerned with a paring away of unnecessary complexities in this strategy, along with an almost didactic reinforcement in consciousness of everyday tactics of keeping out of trouble, in the sense of major social invalidation.[24] The mode of operation of therapy—and when I talk of therapy I am talking about all of us as therapists, insofar as we are the continuing dyad of therapist/therapeutized (although the therapist movement has to be disciplined for a wider social use in some selected, not elected, people)—consists in the recollecting of several connections that at least does not deprive the person of a freedom to reconnect things in her or his own way. The work of therapy, for the therapist, resides very centrally in the negative praxis of not depriving, based on the realization that *in this context* of relationship no-one can deprive anyone of anything anyhow. The guilty therapist feels all the time that he is not giving enough, but the "crime" is centered in the guilt and not in the giving or not giving. The most destructive consequences of therapy arise when the therapist worries about

24 I mean trouble with the neighbors, then the police, then psychiatrists.

himself disguised as the other. The therapeutic change moves through the phase of the therapist, firstly, in which he neither disguises himself nor resorts to a classical absence. After a while, during which the whole thing may fluctuate while the therapist finds his ground, a meeting between the two people becomes possible, and the binary role system of therapist/therapeutized, analyst/*anal*ized, doctor/doctored, breaks down in the full phase of *therapeia.* The "while" this comes after is generated as a time, not in either person, but in the region between persons, which is generated by them in the full interplay of their personal time systems.

But someone comes along to the therapist with "neurotic symptoms," or "early or latent psychotic symptoms," organized with varying degrees of articulateness into some linguistically coherent expression of distress, of fear in any of its recognized modes. If the person is sophisticated enough, he makes sure that he does not fall into the psychiatric stereotype of being "phobic" in a certain prescribed way or "paranoid" in any of its five or six or fifty or six hundred variants of expression. So he decides, through a certain choice of language structures, to talk of feelings he has had in the street about strangers reacting to his presence with subtly communicated thoughts about his being queer or, in some more diffuse sense, mad, or he decides to talk in terms of the reverberations or waves or resonances or kinesic alterations that he receives from other people, in any situation, about the ways that he "comes on to" them. This is his problem. At this stage of history, the conventionally trained psychiatrist is already defeated and the conventionally trained psychoanalyst has to go back to do some homework. Conventional interpretative models based on inner-outer relations—introjection-splitting-projection-reintrojection—are always serviceable, but it is only a very ancient, etymological tracing back of *therapeia* (which in one sense means "serving" the other) that makes servicing central to therapy. Nor is serving any longer socially relevant, except as an intensification of invalidation.[25] Nor "ministering," which is finally prefixed with the "ad."

But let us not minimize the problem here. Someone comes along with "neurotic" symptoms, and these are not without a devious and perhaps urgent reality. The reality centers on a desperate impulse to maintain a survival purchase on the normal world, without which one seems to be in a required abnegation of a pristine personal reality that the person has just begun to feel his way back to.

Someone came to see me with a list of symptoms that, in recounting, amounted to seven in number. This person had some recollection of a myth that seemed to fit the numbering of his seven "dis-eases." The myth was of a group, a body of seven bespectacled wise men who, instead of lenses, had mirrors before their eyes. It is easy, by a facile etymologizing, to regard symptoms as a falling together; it requires just a little more effort, but perhaps a lot of therapy, to see an original togetherness that simply could not believe in itself until it found a mirror or series of mirrors in the recesses of itself, built out of nothing but the immaterial matter of itself. Symptoms, in fact, are a self-inspecting mode of dismembering one's self, but at this stage the self is falsely substantialized as a goal of some sort —one has to be or become one's own self.

One examiner of psychiatrists for the Diploma in Psy-

25 In certain mental hospitals in England, it is the custom on Christmas day for doctors to visit "their" wards and serve dinner to "their" patients who, a few hours later, will once again become "chronic dilapidated schizophrenics." The irony here is that there is some reality of feeling in this bathetic exchange. There is a tiny glimmer of warmth that is snuffed out in less feudal "therapeutic communities."

chological Medicine used to ask candidates why schizophrenics looked in mirrors so much. The expected answer was, "to make sure that they are really there." In fact, what people who risk being called schizophrenic do with mirrors is to attempt to see through the social appearance of the self, the self for others, into the nothingness that is the reality of one's self for oneself. The mirror-gazing is not a false project to reassure oneself about a sense of ontological insufficiency, of not being there enough in the world; on the contrary, it is an effort *not* to see oneself any more, to see through oneself as a person limited to relative being, circumscribed by referent others. Few people can sustain this nonrelative self-regard for more than a minute or two without feeling that they are going mad in the sense of disappearing. That is why people use mirrors in order not to see their selves with the possibility of seeing through, but to see fragmentary manifestations like their hair, eye make-up, the alignment of their tie and so on. If one did not effect this evasive fragmentation of the mirror image, one would be left with the experience of knowing that seeing oneself means seeing through oneself. There can be nothing more terrifying than that.

If one sees one's life as a linear trajectory—out of some past, through the present, heading towards a future—one may be deluded (a normal delusion that madmen are deprived of) into conceiving that there is a goal at some ultimate point on this line that gives the trajectory a topographical definition amongst other "life lines" or social "world lines," and thus gives meaning to our lives.

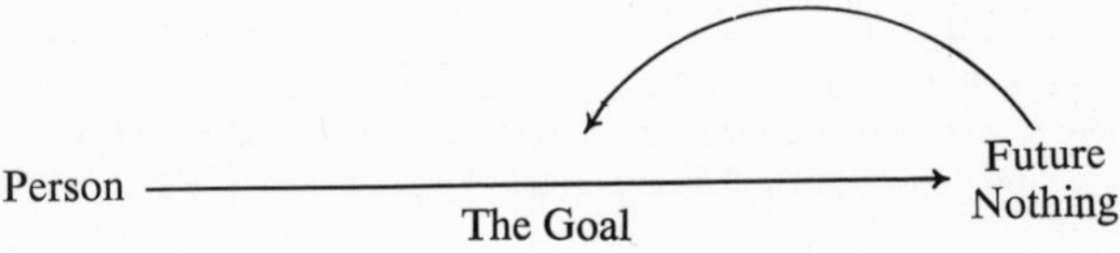

What we do is to seize on a piece of the nothingness of our future and convert it into a quasi-concrete goal object lying on the trajectory of our life, thus effectively blocking our vision by our very desperation to see. We then live by this reified, hypostasized false end and, insofar as we live by it, we die of it. Any meaning derived from a source outside our acts murders us. Perhaps we have then to settle for meaning as being, quite simply, nothing but the nothingness of the geometric point on our life trajectory where we are at this moment. Maybe God has enough problems on his hands without taking on ours, and least of all ours about him, as some sort of bank-managerially approved guarantor of the goals of our lives—in fact, God's biggest problem, if we can be compassionate enough to entertain the possibility, might be his problem about not being God. Maybe the trajectory is nothing more than the flight of the pebble that *we* have thrown into the pool that is us—we are certainly not as substantial as the pebble that we try to be, but conceivably we are the throwing of it, and certainly we are some moment of its flight. To shift the metaphor, we may be the place that no longer exists where Hokusai's tidal wave[26] came from. "We" throw a pebble in the pool which is "us." The stone sinks to the bottom. We are "the sinking to the bottom," and we are the ripples (the tidal waves) that reach out from the point of contact between the stone and the surface of the pool that is no longer there, because the pebble has left it for a place where we are not at either (the bottom of ourselves). A true phenomenology of physical science must be concerned with the appearance of action and the disappearance of objects. A true phenomenology of the self is based on the realization of its

26 The Japanese painter Hokusai's well-known picture of a *tsunami,* or tidal wave.

nonappearance, issuing in critical experiences of absence. To put it another way, the self is always the place where we have come from and go towards, but the appearance of our coming is the disappearance of the place which is always left without existence in the past, in the future and, most evidently, in the present.

The realization of the nonsubstantiality of the self is at the base of what is probably the most radical and transforming experience in "therapy," the experience of the essential irony at the center of some of the most agonizing personal predicaments one may get into. The two levels that define this mode of irony are firstly the level of a full, suffering recognition of "the problem," secondly that what matters is only this recognition of the problematic, and not the immateriality, of the self that afflicts itself with the problem. The problem has to be seen, but inextricably wound up with the seeing of the problem is the seeing through of the self. And so one laughs and laughs with the other who sees through one's self and sees through one's seeing through of one's self. The pain remains totally real, but can now become the ball of a joyous ball game without loss of its value as pain. The joke that the ironic consciousness pushes through into a simultaneously explosive and implosive reality depends on the conjoint recognition of the absurdity of the notion of a self being afflicted by pain. Certainly one can be painfully affected by another person, but in a sense this is straightforward enough and in a sense it is no problem—at least one knows where one is. The problematic, more mystifying and difficult, that I am referring to here is dependent on the idea of one afflicting one's self with the problem. In terms of self-regard, we are *relational beings.* If *relative beings* are people who give priority to the others' regard of them over against their regard of themselves, relational beings give priority to a false otherness in themselves over against the true self-sameness of their selves. We reflect on ourselves so that there is the reflecting self and the self the reflecting self reflects on, and of course one can reflect on the reflecting self, and reflectively decide to cancel it out and simultaneously decide to cancel out the decision as such. The final effect of this common enough gyration is to produce an illusory single self that is something like an object buffeted around the world in a football game that is totally passive and totally joyless. Through some ironic recognition, however, one can ask the question, "Who is the self afflicted by this problematic, and who is the self that afflicts itself in this manner?" And then one can ask a further question: "And what is the difference between these two selves anyhow?" If one asks this question in the only way it can be asked, that is, paradoxically and with fully self-loving and playful absurdity, one simultaneously annihilates it, and this is the ironic liberation into true self-unity.

In short, we have to learn to play with pain. Otherwise we repeat endless, boring games, both with others and inside ourselves. Therapy is about the unplaying of these games and the unasking of questions that are always obreptive lies. Pain is not devalued by this ironic handling of it, but joy is pushed into some almost astrological conjunction with pain. *In terms of the life of a person, irony is the most revolutionary sentiment of all.*

Every infant, needless to say, knows all about this. Each child loves itself enough to play with its pain, until we teach it our games. If we now look into the cradle of the next unending revolution of our times, we will find that our marching song is a *berceuse.* But that's a song we have to listen to before we begin singing it. The fallen state of falling asleep is as disastrous as falling in love. The falling is counterrevolutionary in the fullest sense. We have to sleep and awaken and love. So one falls in various states of intoxication at some point at least approximating love, and is bruised for it, or maybe with some luck loved for it. But at some point a separateness has to prevail, so that the quasi-monogamous couple opens itself up to the world. All monogamy is a pretense at being what it is. An unpretending act may both produce a cessation of the pretense and initiate, in a way that I would designate revolutionary, the beginning of Love and the birth of the bomb—but not That Bomb.

# The Love and Madness Revolution

THE MOST PREVALENT FEAR, for the most part secret or ill-expressed or unexpressed in first-world societies, is the fear of a madness that knows no limits—madness that shatters the prestructured life not only of one person, the person who "goes mad," but beyond that a whole social region of life. For everyone who knows that person or who knows someone who does, the fantasy runs on: the world will go to pieces, we shall all go to pot, all our minds blown out, uselessly and finally. There can be no time limit to think about what is going on. *Their* madness becomes a common property, it is *our* madness, and the ensuing problem is how best we can relegate our madness to a safe place, i.e., a place where that "other" is put away, safely containing our madness for us, somewhere else.

Mental breakdowns, psychosis, schizophrenia, are supposed to go on for some time. The time, with full irony, is medically prescribed. "It" goes on for weeks, months or years. With successful treatment, it is only a matter of two or three weeks or months. A few electric shocks, a few pills (at a profit, on tranquilizers, estimated at 1,000 per cent to the drug industry) can reduce this to the minimum figure. Otherwise it takes a bit longer to knock this or that person into socially acceptable shape. We should not forget that doctors and surgeons came from barbers, the people who shave scalps into the right tonsure—or the wrong one. But above all, celibacy is demanded.

The movement is always out of fucking and into eating. Lethal syphilis remains in India, but in the nineteenth-century West we die of our consumption. Our consumption, our consuming, is our disease—the label is fully written out.

I have never known one person who did not go fully into his particular madness and come out of it within about ten days, given a certain lack of interference in the guise of treatment. If one other person could stay with the person who is supposed to be going through the madness experience, without calling for help in any suspect mode, I would think that the person going into madness would naturally work through his experience and then maybe come back for further elucidation, but not necessarily so. The only problem in real, effective terms is how to keep out of the way of the bin, which might be either the conventional mental hospital or its even more grotesque successor, the advanced general hospital psychiatric unit, where all the "diseases" are treated equally. The "unit" is the eunuchizer of the system and, with full state subsidization, it works as a subsidizing of itself into a factory of nonminds.

First-world society is, of course, a consumer society. Second-world society, of course, with some theoretical Marxist-Leninist qualifications of what it is about, aspires to the same fate. By some curious quirk of history, the most lethal disease of imperializing Europe was called consumption (tuberculosis), even "galloping consumption" if it got bad enough and near enough to death—with the terminal euphoria expressing the content that expressed the quietistic view that nothing real was happening: "I'm dying, but I'm consumed by a bacillus from my insides, so don't worry, hang on, wait." This disease transected class divisions: one could be a chimney sweep or a soldier in South Africa or a major writer, but one died of the disease that gave birth to the first world. And, through the decades, Keats had it, Katherine Mansfield had it, Simone Weil had it, *you* too can have it. Have it and be had by it, live and die of it.

Country A (say, the United States of America) buys tomatoes from country B (say, one impoverished South American state), and it sells them back, in tins, to country B at 300 percent profit. This is known as "aid," and aid comes very close to help and treatment, all three being ways of keeping the social world in good order, either on the personal or on the macrosocial level.

The emotional sense of fascism, at this point in time, is terrifyingly extended. It is no longer simply a matter of militia and police and secret police operating violently against people in the interest of monopoly capitalism in crisis. The most benevolent institutions of our society become our oppressors, in a way that relegates the gas chambers of Auschwitz to the level of a naive, fumbling attempt at massacre; the last expiring, cyanidized breath is only the beginning of torture. Techniques of annihilating bodies, of course, lead on to techniques of annihilating minds, and this whole region of *technē* has a platitudinous quality by now. The real horror of it, though, is that when it comes to minds no-one reminds himself to mind. If the tortures of bodies are incidentally unminded, the unminded unmindness of the assassins of thought and feeling is quite central to the nature of their lethal work. We live on into and generate, and are generated by, an age of benevolent care. Everyone worries about the fate of Czechoslovak anti-Stalinism, but no-one is concerned enough about himself to perceive—let alone protest against—the computerized checking operation about every aspect of his life. So we are centralized into a false state, which is "the" State.

What the true state is we shall leave in parenthesis (and it may have to remain there), but let us stay with the false state that is the State. The Chancellor of the Exchequer is a good psychiatrist—he diagnoses a certain state of affairs and then introduces regulators that control incomings and outgoings. What he does not know is that when he talks about the financial management of the country's economy, he is talking with absolute (and absolutely inexperienced) primacy about a certain tension in the masculature of his arsehole. He has forgotten his body or lost his body in the body politic. Every word he says about the balance of payments is poised, not on the lip of his mouth, but on the lip of his anus, words slipping through piles of painful, thrombosed, stagnant blood hidden in the folds of an overdone political steatopygy. No wonder that young people, to separate the folds and get a clear view of the hidden darkness, think in terms of setting alight the ballot boxes. But on one day every year this Chancellor manages to produce an ancient black brief case containing, not a healthy shit joyously evacuated, but a retained turd that is exhibited for TV cameramen trying to get the budget into public vision and then withdrawn into the dark, succulent, colonic recesses of his mind (that is no longer his mind but a pitiable collective nonmind that never matters through a series of negations of every social act that might make some difference to some actual person). The ultimate defense employed by English imperialism is that of innocence; to unknowingly show what it does not know, and then hope for the best and supply arms and a manual of good-enough bluff. The theological justification of this no doubt comes from Martin Luther, who felt himself to be a turd in God's arsehole waiting to be shitted into the world and then, with a pure assumption of passivity, waited for the other person to do the shitting. Well, maybe the shit will come and maybe the "other people" will do it. And maybe Grosvenor Square or the Place Saint-Michel or Central Park, New York, or the whole of the city of Chicago won't be chamber pots of adequate capacity to contain the excrement without spilling.

In Cuba, they hope to abolish money in ten years. Everyone will be able to walk into shops and help themselves to whatever they need without paying, or get into trains or buses and travel anywhere without fares. Everyone will be as greedy or as abstemious as he needs as long as his appetite is true. In the meantime, every woman, man and child in Cuba has access to a gun because they know that in Miami there are many people with lying appetites, people who are conditioned single-mindedly to take and consume and not see how they are consumed by their consumption.

The skin is another very difficult region of covertly corporealized sociopolitical experience. I am talking, of course, about immigration policy. Through the thickening calluses of our political pachydermy, we have lost touch with the nerve endings that convey touch to us and let us be touched, because we are afraid of becoming "touched" by our touching. In England, the skin barrier is critical; there, our certain "black" "heads" must be allowed no purchase on the soil of our evidently soilable cutaneity.

Keep the black bits out of our body and keep our minds white and pure—but be "fair" while we get the black bits out. Thus speaks the anonymous collective voice of a society that has never expurgated itself in the sense of sweating it out through the pores of its social skin, through its pores, or poorness. A society that has never discovered its own poverty but has always pushed it out into the third world. Stanley and Livingstone shake "hands" across Africa, in a mutual masturbation that denies the world in a sadistic exclusivity. Biafra is invented to suffer, and the imperializing consciousness is lost in Zimbabwe after losing thousands of nonfantasy people in the prison camps, or on the gallows erected out of a strong family love by our fair kith and kin. Hundreds of paranoid policemen are mobilized from their family weekends to beat up dissenters in Grosvenor Square or imprison the communards of Piccadilly, but not one of them is sent to cast out Smith—pregnant with his covertly incestuous child—onto the wintry plains and Christmas snows of Zimbabwe. This must surely be family love at its reckless limit. But then, even the most secure families crumble when someone longs hard enough not to belong and generates sufficient revolutionary counterviolence to destructure the mendacious structure and introduce a saboteur truth. At this point I find a subtle but luminous equation of madness and political victory.

In a sense, all we have to do first, in our first-world context, is to liberate ourselves personally by a Madness Revolution. If this liberation is radical enough within us and extensive enough over the whole society, it will mean that the first world becomes ungovernable and that its internal power structure will disintegrate, and consequently, that its external power, represented by imperialist violence against the third world, will no longer operate.

We can perhaps talk about "madness," which is the genocidal and suicidal irrationality of the capitalist mode of governing people, and "Madness," which is the individual tentative on the part of actual, identifiable people to make themselves ungoverned and ungovernable—not by undisciplined spontaneity, but by a systematic reformation of our lives that refuses aprioristic systematization but moves through phases of destructuring, unconditioning, de-educating and de-familializing ourselves, so that we at last get on familiar but unfamilial terms with ourselves and are then ready to restructure ourselves in a manner that refuses all personal taboos and consequently revolutionizes the whole society.

All we have to do about the first world is to stop it. We shall stop it by passing beyond the pale of our skin color and by entering into a free metamorphosing of color and recognizable form in a political kaleidoscope of deadly play. Amongst other colors, we shall turn black and red. Amongst other forms, we shall turn mad, but no longer dead.

Raoul Vaneigem was right when he wrote: *"Ceux qui parlent de révolution . . . sans se réferer explicitement à la vie quotidienne . . . ont dans la bouche un cadavre."*[27]

Unless we are overly fond of the corpse we consume and are infatuated with the taste of our death, we must spit it back in the face of the system that would cremate us, so that even Artaud's desperate symbol of our predicament—we, all of us, signaling mutely through the flames of our respective pyres to each other—is no longer possible.

In a system that defines itself by the negation of the negation, the system that says no to every person and

27 "Those who speak of revolution . . . without making it real in their own daily lives . . . talk with a corpse in their mouths!" *Traité de savoir-vivre à l'usage des jeunes générations* (Paris: Gallimard, 1967), p. 19.

every experience that would be born and borne without becoming *borné* at the quick of its life, the hyphenated system of capitalist state—bourgeois family–policemen–psychiatrist, it is perhaps surprising that few people can be so ruthless that they are generous enough to say "No!" But then, if we prise open the surprise, we may undertake the surprise as a false sentiment that simply reflects the mystification of the system that operates always at a second remove from the primary experience. This is the preconditioned base of all game structures between persons and is the social base of the structures of repression (Freud) and bad faith (Sartre)—the latter being a socially extended, reconceived version of the former that does not rely on an objectlike unconscious. In this sense, all the games we play with each other are capitalist games. Introspection is a bourgeois habit. But we all want to win. But we even more want to be "won over" (passivity) by being "one over" (activity). The happiest fate, the fate of the Glad Man, is to drift into activity. The ultimate desire of the man who would be glad is to fuck the world, not with his penis, which could never be quite big enough, nor with some other metaphorized potency, but with something else less clearly detachable from him—in either mode of so-called castration, either someone taking his prick away from him, or someone taking him away from his thrusting phallus.

Well, why not the nose? One of the most usual problems in therapy with men is that they have at least two noses. One nose, that comes from Mother, is grafted on to an original "biological" nose. In a culture dominated by the need to be strong in a way that becomes socially visible as phallic strength, even mothers need penises. If Father takes his penis away and loses it in work, in casual fucks or solitary masturbation, and if the whole person of the mother's son cannot become her schizophrenic penis, she is left with the son's internalization of her that gets pushed out to somewhere like the tip of his nose. Ironically, in a favorite meditation exercise one is supposed to concentrate one's ego in one's nose and then let it fall off the tip so that one is launched into anegoic liberation. What usually happens is that one's internal mother falls off the tip and comes back for more of the self that is patently still all there.

So the internal family goes on and is externally reflected in all our relationships. The internal problematic is that, like God, fathers have to be invented for want of their existence, and that, once again like God, mothers have to become dead for wanting existence—someone else's. None of this may be necessary at all, but we spend most of our time, directly or indirectly, knowingly or unknowingly, in this sort of exercise. Of course, the only problem is how we manage to be nice and kind to each other and then possibly a bit more, but few of us seem to reach the first rung of this ladder of undoing the false problematic.

The nose that knows is not the apparent nose (the family nose) that thinks it knows what the nose really knows. The gnosis of the nose is a capacity of the secret, second nose that knows of the no-ing of the nose that it is. The first nose, the transplant, is pure affirmation that knows it dare not know anything at all. The gnosis that is the second nose knows that noses don't really know anyhow and certainly know nothing of no-ing, in the sense of saying "no" generously to anyone about either a presented fantasy that is concerned with noses or with noses that are not gnosis.

Talking about fathers, Freud said:

> Let us agree, therefore, that the great man influences his contemporaries in two ways: through his personality and through the idea for which he stands. . . . Sometimes—and

> this is surely the more primitive effect—the personality alone exerts its influence and the idea plays a decidedly subordinate part. Why the great man should rise to significance at all we have no doubt whatever. We know that the great majority of people have a strong need for authority which it can admire, to which it can submit, and which dominates and sometimes even ill-treats it. We have learned from the psychology of the individual whence comes this need of the masses. It is the longing for the father that lives in each of us from his childhood days, for the same father who the hero of legend boasts of having overcome. And now it begins to dawn on us that all the features with which we furnish the great man are traits of the father, that in this similarity lies the essence—which so far has eluded us—of the great man.[28]

But what is this father? The true violence is that children are placed in the desperate position of needing "fathers," violent fathers. Someone who was brought up in a working-class area of Manchester by Communist Party parents who were distinctly upper-class, Spock-enlightened academics heard enviously of a friend who had been violently thrashed by his father for saying "damn." When he told his father to "fuck off," he was told: "You should never speak to your father like that when other people are here." Fortunately, the upper-class family broke up, but the son had not had much luck with other people since then.

A girl aged five years was the daughter of a medical missionary in northern India. Her father had been away for over a month, being a "family doctor" over a large area. When he returned, the girl was in a frenzy of excitement about seeing him again and came all over him in a way he simply could not stand, because of the sexual overtones and the presented prospect of untamed joy. He raised his hand to hit her and quiet her, but checked the blow six

28 *Moses and Monotheism* (New York: Knopf, 1939, pp. 172–73; London: Hogarth Press, 1939, pp. 173–74).

inches short of its object. Instead, he and her mother got together and decided to put her to bed for one week until she "came down." She did. Twenty-one years later she again became ecstatic in relation to her husband and two children. For one brief afternoon she enjoyed herself, played tricks with language and felt deliciously happy. Again the hand was raised. Again it never came down, and she was put to bed for a week in a local mental hospital. Electroconvulsive treatment was discussed, but she never even had that false, punitive gratification. She had not been bad enough, just too happy, so she came down instead of coming out, with tranquilizers. The father-husband and the father-doctor arranged her readmission on the five subsequent occasions when she became too high or too happy, until she finally decided to leave home and live alone. All homes are family homes. The family, as we have seen, is endlessly replicated in its anti-instinctuality throughout all the institutions of this society. Leaving home is the shortest possible answer. This girl could only tell her story about the original nontrauma with her father years after she had left the mental-hospital system where the story could never be heard because it challenged the family structure of the hospital too deeply.

The prostitute is someone who stands for someone else, bits and pieces of the minds and bodies of our parents and siblings and our parents' parents and our own children. The good brothel is a family scene where all our incestuous and polymorphous-perverse fantasies can be enacted and held by us in such a manner that the taboos and fears of sexuality within the family system are transcended with discipline, time regulation, and fee structure and beyond that, some dignity.

In the second chapter of this book I defined love as based on a correct act of establishing separateness. Sexuality, which is directed into love from above and below, from before and after, is very much a matter of learned technique and none of us is beyond learning a bit more. The making public, or at least visible within the context of a two-person relationship, of our most feared fantasies can be liberating beyond words. For example, many men and women are afraid of masturbating while simply being watched without direct participation of the other. Also, simple fantasies like the wish to be urinated on by the other seem too fearful to be announced.

The psychiatrist would be a prostitute (this chapter could well be entitled "Portrait of the Psychiatrist as a Young Prostitute") on the level of the *technē* of how we are to live. To do this, he has also to learn about standing in as someone else of any sex or age for someone else. Most psychiatrists are inexperienced or "young" in this ancient technique of working with persons on the issue of what they are doing with their lives. It is fairly easy to fall into being a father figure, but that is only the beginning of the story. Certain European communes state as their theoretical *prise de position* the abolition of the father, the replacement of a paternal ideal by a fraternal one. What they do, in fact, is to reinvent families with a quasi-legalistic proscription of relationship possibilities, and sometimes an actual legal definition of relationship in which a contract is drawn up between two people with a lawyer to provide, in particular, for the woman and her children. The costly pay-off here is that the whole thing is not called marriage.

To get back to the problem that the psychiatrist has, it seems to me that there is a rigidification of role that reflects a certain social sclerosis. The psychiatrist is propelled into being a father figure, with some elements of mother figure added to this initial pro-stitution. It is very much more difficult for him to feel childlike in relation to "his" "patient." If he does, he falls into the trap of seeing the other person as parental superego who would control his life punitively. It is even more difficult to fall into the position that I believe to be the most fundamentally important position in psychotherapy: that of the ancient, bisexual man-woman who at certain critical points explodes into a serious joke.

One young man, who announced to me on introduction that he was "a homosexual" (the label, of course, giving a certain security of self-definition), gave me to read a letter to him from his mother. The letter was about her heart bursting (she had been hospitalized on several occasions with heart attacks[29]) when she visited Lake Geneva, which he had told her was his "soul place." As I read the letter, which was evidently a love letter with the passion pushed out, I felt a transformation in my relation to the young man in the sense that I became his mother more than his internal mother was his mother. The intonation of my voice altered, became higher, with a distinctly *Urmutter* quality, while his voice sank into a subdued masculine sound. We had invented parents all over again, but the point of change was that, in reading his mother's letter, I felt the progressive extrusion of his internalized mother into me, not as a theoretical construct, but in actual experience.

He was left with the faint appearance of his father. Bit by bit, in subsequent sessions, he realized his fear of his

29 The metaphor of "attack" is widespread in medicine. One suffers an attack of biliary colic or influenza. In treatment, the same metaphor is continued: one attacks leukemia or other forms of cancer, or cerebral syphilis, with treatments that are themselves diseases. The medical strategies of therapeutic attack seem to leave out not only the liberal possibilities of peaceful coexistence, say, with one's cancer but also the more liberating possibility of loving one's dis-ease and inviting it to live with one in a sort of antimarriage that might break down the statistical reduction of certain cancers to two- or five- or seven-year survival rates after surgery or radiotherapy. In an extreme statement, one might say that all lethal diseases are suicide in the sense of a refusal to love.

father's fear of his (the father's) love for him. This became concretized in his fantasy as a sexual-aggressive equation in which he would be fucked–assaulted–masculinized by an orgasmic penetration of "the man" in a wished-for LSD session with me.

The illusory nature of this man's wish was quickly seen through, but if, as in most cases, psychiatrists are arrested on the same level of aspiration, then the violence of psychiatric treatment truly commences. The "other," containing the madness of the community, has to be silenced in the guise of care or even an anti-Pauline "conversion." One illuminating bit of the horror story is the diagnosis and treatment of "homosexuals" by aversion methods. Men whom the psychiatrists complain are complaining of homosexual wishes have a gadget attached to their penises that measures the strength of erection by the blood volume in the penis. They are shown a series of nude men interspersed with a series of nude women. When they respond to the nude men by erectile increase, they are given an electric shock; when they respond to nude women, they are given the "reward" of nonshock. It has been estimated that around seventy percent of homosexual men "convert" after their experience. Not one word is mentioned about the attitude of the investigator to his own homosexuality, to the reaction any person has to pain induced by electric shock, or above all, to the quality of the nude photographs. All that seems to matter is that in the end one submits to stop the painful shocks. The criterion of successful psychiatric treatment is once again seen to be submission to the dominant values of the society. Any respectable prostitute would be more respectful than this. But psychiatrists are not yet respectable prostitutes. Psychiatrists, by virtue of their training, tend to be formed into identical men in the same pin stripe clothing, with the same carefully tied shoelaces, the same expressions of cordiality, the same English public school or Central European accents, and the same garrote around their necks that gets tied around the necks of their patients, which are both their necks and the necks of the factory-farmed chickens in their local butcher shops. It is small wonder that Cerletti invented electroconvulsive treatment under the spell of the abattoirs of Rome—the inspiration of the personality transformation of half-slaughtered pigs is the leitmotif of the soap opera of contemporary psychiatry.

At the same point in the first six months after birth, the following critical situation may arise in certain babies. At first the baby cries with what is the same cry as its mother, although of course it is usually the *uncried* cry of the mother that the baby cries with. There is a certain continuum of mood between mother and child that can be symbiotically perpetuated indefinitely even into adult life, leaving many of us in an emotional no man's land in which we are in a state of not crying the uncried distress feeling of another (mother). But then the mother may demonstrate an instinctive capacity to be separate from her baby by not going automatically to stop the baby crying. She shows a capacity to contain her own disturbance and let the baby have its own. In this case, she may become aware of a change in the quality of the baby's cry. It becomes no longer her cry, or rather *their* cry, but the baby's *own* cry. In some sense both will always know and remember if this experience happens, and its historical event should certainly become evident in therapy.

In my view this happening is somewhat rare, and for want of it we find a great deal of compulsive gregariousness. For instance cocktail parties, which are personally atomized but socially collective—the atomized collective as distinct from the face-to-face "confrontation group" in which people relate to each other from autonomous positions.

The noise generated at a cocktail party is more than the sum of the voices that speak, and the most apt characterization that I can think of for that sound is the desperation in each person to find his own cry, the cry he was deprived of which he cannot find *with* other people, but in some desolate region *through* other people. Thus, many people go to parties in a search for a correct solitude, but inevitably get lost on the way because they are unclear of their need and would never imagine that they go to the party in order not to be there. So the true solitude is lost in a frenetic loneliness.

One can perhaps define a party that is *not* like this, in the sense that solitude is made more real so that people talk freely from the depths of an inner order that makes no demands on another person and is therefore the pure gift of the *abyssus invocat abyssum.* The people who come to the party would then be related in this way: two people who had never met before might get talking, but there would be a prior sense of connection in that one of the two people would have had a significant experience with someone that the other person would have had a significant experience with, or perhaps at one remove from that, but no further. This "prior connection" does not limit spontaneity but in fact conditions the possibility of its appearance in the occasion. I am not suggesting the conversion of the party into some sort of austere work situation, but I am saying that work and a certain discipline are necessary in this situation and that the joy that might be enjoyed emerges from this prior work. As opposed to the conventional ideal of "looking for new relationships" with an inexorable quality of desperation, I am suggesting a dialectical move back into old relationship structures that simultaneously moves into a new region. Part of the "party work," needless to say, would include the free developing of open sexual relating in any form, with the careful respect of anyone's right to say no without this being taken as rejection.

By significant experience I mean any act, even though this may be momentary in time, of total attentiveness and total registration of each person by the other. This could take the form of one person seeing a painting, hearing some improvised music or reading a manuscript by the other. Or it could be a sexual relationship in which some body taboos were broken down, or it could be a session in which a drug like cannabis was used in a coolly liberating way, or it could be in some formally defined therapeutic encounter—or again, some occasion not formally defined in which one person has looked after the other at a time of distress or bodily need.

One great limitation on the effective operation of radical political groups is that these elementary acts of communion are either fragmented or simply not recognized, and instead one has an infinitely multiplying complex of quasi-incestuous relationships that evade—rather than resolve—the old problems of incest and perpetuate sexual blocks that conceal a mounting but unusable fury. Liberation must end on the revolutionary battle field, but must also start in bed. The bed, here, is the bed one is born in, sleeps and dreams in and makes love in. Guns have their place, of course, but the bed is perhaps the great unused secret weapon of the revolution that we have to do.

After revolutionaries, madmen. At one psychiatric aftercare hostel that costs the local authority a great deal of money, the discharged patients from the local mental hospital are sexually segregated and the door between the male and female wings can be opened but has an electronic eye. If someone should try to cross this threshold after a certain hour, a bell rings in the bedroom of the warden, who of course sleeps (at least) with his properly married wife. For many people who are hospitalized as schizophrenic the main problem is the mystifying presentation of sexual fear by their parents in a way that caricatures the diffuse sexual fear of the whole bourgeois society.

When I once ran a unit for young men called schizophrenic within the National Health Service structure, the pathos of sexual deprivation was quite incredible. One young man went to London to visit a prostitute, and shortly afterwards his transfer to a locked ward in another hospital was skillfully manipulated by his parents after he had spent a weekend at home with them and had been so conditioned by them into keeping no secrets that he told the truth. George Washington—that unlying man—has a great deal to answer for. As far as families are concerned, one of the main learning experiences in therapy must be the acquisition of an adequate capacity to lie, because if one tells the right lie one tells the truth of the mendacious system.

The so-called sexual desegration of mental hospitals is simply a further mystification, in a sort of clinical prick-teasing, that will only further imprison its victims. In the case of the unit I have referred to, I suggested, as a way of rapidly saving the National Health Service money, the employment of one or two experienced men or women (this was an all-male ward) who would act as temple prostitutes and sexually initiate the young men—paid overtime for so-called perversions, if necessary. Technique is quite central to sexuality, but sexuality is the most feared object of the psychiatric service, which needs it madmen and is terrified of losing its unreasonable *raison d'être.* So the outpatient clinics multiply, as do the variety of tranquilizer drugs, as do the literal or metaphorical electronic eyes that, in the interest of some remote and crazy family ideal, destructively control every ecstatic possibility of experience and any tentative to sexual liberation.

Most tranquilizers make people fat and impotent but indubitably tame. In fact, the patient becomes the psychiatrist's systematically degraded alter ego.

Behind the facility of Wordsworth's dictum, "Poetry is emotion recollected in tranquillity," there lies a not unimportant truth. Memory implies an analytic dismemberment of certain regions of experience and then recognizes certain *modes* of the dismemberment, which is the analytic operation. The discipline here gets inevitably into and often caught up in verbal language. Repression, in Freud's sense, is very much about experience that is "pushed out" of mind and has to find its way back into known experience through the barbed-wire entanglements of words. Recollection, on the other hand, is an essentially extraverbal act of collecting one's life together into one piece by actually experiencing again some of the very earliest experiential moments of one's life. The discipline in this case, and it is as strong as in the case of memory, is not analytic (the definition of sectors of experience and the definition of boundaries of sectors and interrelations across and through these boundaries), but rather it is poetic. The tranquillity is important, as this means a right solitude, the solitude of the first six months that I have been talking about, either physically alone or in the presence of another who may catalyze the development but never interferes. The true poet knows that words, on the deepest level, are irrelevant to his experience, that is, the recollecting of himself so that in fact he generates a violence against language that tweaks the nose of words and then inserts a pig ring into them and leads them by it into the reality of his recollected experience. *If poets are athletes of the extraver-*

*bal, so are many people called schizophrenic.*

Much psychoanalysis tends to be reductive analysis from verbal structures uttered in the present to preverbal structures that go back to the time in one's life when, quite literally, one could not speak, and then forward again into a resolved present. I believe that there is an extraverbal continuum of experience that runs from points in time that antedate our conception and shoot us into realms way beyond our life-span futures.

Some people called schizophrenic seem to me to operate for much of the time on this extraverbal continuum. So do poets, but poets make a talented concession to the world by dipping back into the Word. The discipline of poetry, and I am talking about *poesis* in the widest sense, including painting and music and other art forms, does not consist in a deployment of letters on paper, paints on canvas, notes on staves or instrumental technique, but in a prior internal operation that *is* the art work.

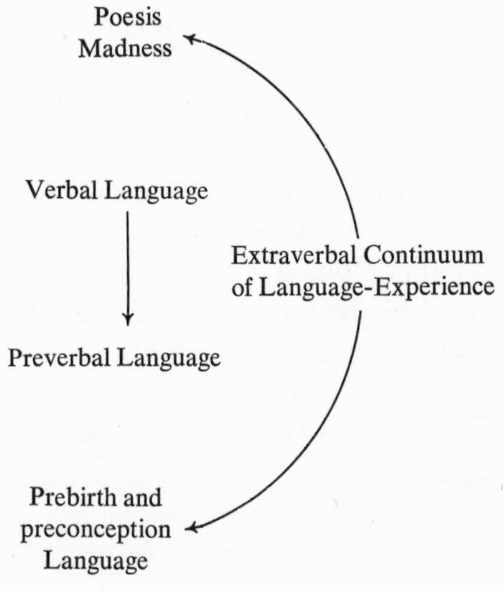

The very recently evolved tradition of touching and holding between people, the new tradition of hugging and kissing anyone on every encounter, not just on socially prescribed meetings, seems to me to be good, but essentially a desexualizing, anti-erotic maneuver. It introduces a warmth, but the freezing plates are turned on underneath to melt the warmth and to limit its extent. If one is going to get on to the transexual reality of orgasm that dialectically retains sexuality in the present new level of synthesis, one has to be open to further moves all the time.

One invention that moves further is "bed therapy," strictly outside the professionally encompassed realm, of course, in which two people who may be stuck in a one-sided and later two-sided sexual withdrawal are held by a third person, who is disciplined enough not to interfere with their relationship but to generate through her or his holding of them, with an intense fondness that he feels for both, their own holding of each other and then leave them to evolve a renewed fucking out of the holding they have achieved. One of them may later do the same for him or her.

Multiple lovemaking may come later, in the sexual need system of some people, through a further acquisition of discipline that again reinforces the central two-person relationship that most of us still seem to need at the present historical moment.

This is all very well for sophisticated first-world middle-class intellectuals who even then, unless charismatically guided, will have their "difficulties," but for the less sophisticated middle-class and working-class men-women relationships (the upper classes being fully and finally dedicated to nonsexuality) one needs a more totally operating revolutionizing activity in the whole society. This is where acutely posed strikes, bombs and machine guns will have to come in, with a guiding compassion but also a certain reality that is wholly objective, seen and felt, by the agents of bourgeois society, towards whom we can only be compassionate at a second remove.

Institutionalized work, hard-drug addiction, alcoholic habituation—after all the personal analysis—come down to some sort of subtly indoctrinated effort to contain an ecstatic joy that might not "marry" the bombs but get into a full, free union with them. All we have to do with the first-world structure, the structure that destroys the third world and has a paranoid, suspicious, illicit union with the second world, is to stop it. We have to paralyze the functioning of each family, school, university, factory, business corporation, television company, film industry segment—and then, having stopped it, invent mobile, nonhierarchic structures that distribute the accumulated possessions over the whole world. These structures will become rigid in due course, because of of our fearful attitude to our freedom, but if we observe the principle of continuous revolution—the overthrowing of social structures that after a while unknowingly invent their own death and then pre-tend themselves a certain life—we shall find a way, not only to survive, but to never fall back into the normal pattern of the world, which is the only sense of "regression" that one can recognize at this stage of history.

Perhaps the only "true" relationships are those that echo the separation of the crying mother and child. From here, two people come together. From here, the revolution. Sometimes, because of this, one gets closest to a true symbiosis if there are seven thousand miles between oneself and the other person. And then, if one knows one is in it at the depths of oneself, one is out of it, and one cries with one's own cry in one's own unshared wilderness. Good kind friends may try to help, but that is *their* cry in their wilderness. Well, that sort of wilderness, at least, can never be possessed as anyone's territory. One traverses the internal topography of a self that, as we have shown, is an abstraction leading into a nothing that is beyond only insofar as it was so prior to the self that, almost humorlessly, we are talking about.

The main reality that I can perceive in what people regard as orgasm is in terms of a nonpossessive entry into the orgasm of the other. What it is that one becomes is *that* that that is that it is.

Two or three thousand people that I have spoken with over the last decade seem to me to have no articulation of experience that approximates what I would regard as orgasmic experience. Orgasm is the total experience of transexuality. The fucker is fucked in the course of his or her fucking. One becomes not only both sexes but also all ages and all generations in making love. One becomes a blissful infant and also, simultaneously, an ancient bisexual sage. Above all one pours out of oneself, in a massive evacuating act, the whole internalized family constellation. Making love thus becomes the transcendence of the nonfucking of one's parents and the nonlove of families.

In the first-world context I think we need, simultaneously, a Love Revolution that reinvents our sexuality,[30] a Madness Revolution that reinvents our selves, and then Revolution, in terms of a far more direct paralysis of the operations of "the State." In the first world, our revolutionary duty is quite simple. All we have to do, as I have said, is to stop it and enjoy ourselves by taking a dispossessed joy into ourselves in the process.

What I think we have to do, in terms of the first need

30 It is noteworthy that people attain co-orgasm much more freely in casual relationships than they do with the person they live with.

system that I have referred to, is to create the relationship conditions for a noncompetitive lovemaking. All pricks and all cunts are very much the same, except in terms of minutiae of experience—which are also very important. The "ego trip" of comparing sexual experiences is simply irrelevant at this time. All we have to do is to experience, as fully as possible, an ecstatic love in full separateness.

# Death and Revolution

## BLACK CLOTHES

WHY am I in mourning black?
Mourning for the families I had
for the madness I never had
But now allow myself
for the loss of love in the world
for the respective fates of my parents
for the fullest love I've known that
I've destroyed.
Above all I'm mourning in relation
to my own death
which precisely is the death I live doggedly
And I'm mourning over the death of
love in the world
And the nondistinction of death and love
I'm mourning about the nondistinction but also
about an excess of distinctions
I'm mourning about my incapacity to
break through all differentiations in the world
so as to make the cosmos one activity
I'm mourning about the apparent distance
of stars and galaxies because I can't find them
all in one place which is my heart

which is the heart of the world.
I'm mourning that light years between
us and Andromeda are a myth that
people believe. Andromeda is in us and we in it.
I'm mourning about the scarcity of a true
violence that liberates through the killing
of death—a violence that lovingly plants a bomb in
the heart of death.
But above all I'm mourning my own death
But maybe that's another lie
Maybe I'm just mourning
Maybe I'm just
Maybe I may be a being that may be
But maybe I'm just mourning.

Addendum: There may be a certain secret joy in mourning that resides in a quasi-Platonic purity of Idea of "just mourning," which, in the hierarchization of Ideas, ranks somewhere with Love.

I think that if we are to understand mourning, we have to immerse ourselves in realms of experience that are not only prebirth but also before our conception. We also have to consider the after-death experience insofar as we can have this within our lifetime.

There is a particularized mourning that we know a great deal about through the work of Karl Abraham and Melanie Klein. This involves the taking into ourselves of parents that we have destroyed in fantasy by our sadistic attacks on them, with consequent work of reparation. Beyond this form of mourning that is very much *inside* our lives, there is a mourning that goes *beyond* the life span.

I think that Heidegger's *Geworfenheit* is phenomenologically true, true as an experience of being "thrown into the world" by no-one and for no reason, but it is not the whole truth and by no means a holy truth.

I would extend the notion of personal responsibility to

the conditions that precede our conception and the conditions that arise subsequent to our death. Mourning, then, can be about our whole lives encompassed by responsible experience, experience that we have to answer for, before and after the life that we visibly live. There may in fact be a pure living of mourning that is not intelligible in terms of reductive analysis—that is, analysis referring back to early experience after birth, with a view to constructing a practically useful model. This is a mourning that in a sustained manner colors our whole lives black; but then, we know through natural science that black, as well as the absence of light, is really all colors, and all the colors of the world emerge from this blackness—from the blackness of the mourning for a whole personal existence.

Preconception experiences are recollected all the time. We become primal apes, dinosaurs, the first amoebic forms and then inorganic forms all the time without knowing what we are becoming. This is not imagination but actual recollection of our past in the present. We just *do* it and neither see nor remember what we are doing. It's just *there* as the primal places we have come from. By a further act of recollecting we can get a bit further back into the origin of the cosmos (that is, our selves). We do not need LSD to get us there because, if only we knew it, we *are* there. A main function of therapy is to throw a beam of light onto these archaic presences. For instance, certain movements we make can be distinguished clearly as being simian or reptilian or piscine. *At a certain moment, one may be far more truly a monkey than a man.* This, however, is so far removed from everyday consciousness that one has to acquire, through the discipline of therapy, a new mode of noticing, because it is precisely from the region of this archaic complex of presences that we begin to see the entirety of our lives. But to really achieve this entirety of self-vision—which of course does not substantialize our selves but enables us more truly to see through "them"—we have to have a vision from "the other end," the after-death end.

I shall put in parentheses any experience we may have after the biological death of our bodies and leave you to reflect on the Tibetan *Book of the Dead* and the Egyptian *Book of the Dead,* the *De Arte Moriendi* and other medieval writings on the craft of dying.

But I shall concentrate on after-death experiences within the biological life span. These occur in so-called psychosis, in experience called mystical, in dreams and in certain drug states. Also they can occur, rarely, in certain waking states where the person is not engaged in any of the four types of experience that I have expressed above in a hateful language of categorization.

In certain forms of "psychotic" experience there is, at the height of the experience, a pure anoia in which the "outside" becomes continuous with itself through the "inside" so that all sense of self is lost. I shall not dwell on this, as it has been so well described before, particularly in the work of R. D. Laing.

With regard to dreams in relation to the after-death experience, we have to consider how dreams usually terminate, or how their content is suppressed, before the moment of one's death. On the other hand we can have dreams that pursue experience after death within the dream, as a very few people frequently do. One man, a physician, dreamed that he was demonstrating the anatomy of the head to a group of medical students. In the dream he cut off his head and put it on the ground and cut it in half, snot oozing out of its nostrils. He then demonstrated in detail the configuration of the brain (his mind) with fascination and a full sense of understanding. He then calmly kicked the head away, playfully, and walked away further into his death, looking back on the whole of his completed life.

In another dream, the dreamer, again a doctor, was "performing" an autopsy on a cadaver who was himself, aged by at least thirty years. What he did in the dream was to disembowel the cadaver bit by bit and dissect carefully each organ, and then gather all the dissected bits together in his hands and deposit them back into the empty intra-abdominal space and then coarsely sew up the wide autopsy incision that ran from throat to pubis. And then a beautiful young nurse came in and touched the reconstructed dead man in a caring way that got the cadaver to sit up in an enlivened manner, ready to move into a further after-death scene with a simple gratitude and a fleeting but retrospective glance at his whole life.

Dreams like this come close to the shamanistic waking experience of bodily dismemberment followed by ascent into the spirit region and then descent into a reconstituted body, all witnessed by the tribe. These are all modes of real death within biological life, and from the death positions one re-views the entirety of one's life.

After dreams, drugs. One man on an LSD voyage went into a full crucifixion experience. At a certain point he fell across a chair, arms outstretched, to become the cross he (like all of us) was nailed to. His face turned blue, then black, and it was uncertain whether his heart was still beating. Held in the arms of his accompanist, he gradually revived. In the death experience he had had a full vision of his entire life—the future of it as sheer sterility, as well as the past. Two years later, he had an enormously successful exhibition of paintings that seemed to me to be totally antithetic to his previous style of life. This transformation, however, was entirely conditioned by the fact that he had the "right" human accompaniment, and that he had traveled far enough through the unexpectedly present terrain of his death.

In one experience of my own with LSD, I died out of the existence of David Cooper who till then had been alive and well and working in London, and I became a Mongolian sage from about the middle of the nineteenth century. My eyes changed into Mongolian eyes, I grew a long, downwardly pointed mustache and long black hair knotted at the back, and my clothing changed appropriately into his fur-lined robes. He was eating very good Central Asian food with long noodles (whether or not in fact long noodles figure in Central Asian food). The meal that he watched me eat—I think it was *boeuf à la bourguignonne*—turned into small poisonous serpents, and with compassion he watched me die and saw my corpse with perfect detachment. And he witnessed its decomposition. Within the experience, the witnessing seemed important. I felt that no-one should ever be interred and certainly not cremated, but exposed on a bier in a tree for a natural decomposition, to be witnessed by the New Tribe.

The occurrence of after-death experiences in day-to-day waking consciousness is more difficult to define. This evening as I write, in the course of an after-dinner discussion with four very intelligent, sympathetic people I was asked to expound some of my ideas. At a certain pont of disturbance the conversation switched to issues of the institutional work problems that these people were engaged in and then became a defensive chatter that was less and less meaningful to me as the evening progressed. I found myself becoming more and more kinesically frozen and could scarcely think, much less concentrate, unless I distracted myself in the usual way of a Pascalian *diversion.* So without resort to this distraction, I died in the situation. I felt a growing gangrenous process, that I was in some sense in control of, overtake me from the toes and fingers upwards until I reached a point of total bodily putrefaction that I could almost smell and then actually could smell. My external social posture was normal throughout, but at some prefinal point I had a terminal flash back that recuperated all my life and then, while maintaining the normal posture, I momentarily died. I then announced that I was going to bed as I was feeling "unwell," and people decided to leave because of their routine work commitments of the next morning. I was duly composed externally throughout the scene, but the culminating putrefaction was more profoundly real to me in experience than the external manifestation of behavior, because in that present experience the whole past and future enactment of my life was envisaged and totalized from beyond it.

This was certainly a positive experience, but there are also negative modes of entering into a death state within life—negative in the sense that there is no passing through the death state and no re-emergence into life. This is well shown by the relation of true control (discipline) and false control. I know businessmen who drink excessively and yet carry on with "responsible" work. This is false control because it suppresses the reality of feelings of hostility, but more deeply, it suppresses feelings of love. In itself it is usually an indirect aggression against the principal person in that person's life. The effect, however, is to produce a death state within life that amounts to an immense subterranean hatred of the world that is often paraded as love and benevolence and reliability and efficiency and this might fool anyone because the rationalizations are endless. Usually the only way out of this is through a spiritual crisis that may involve the person in some approximation of biological death, for instance, a near-fatal car crash or a severe withdrawal experience with sudden epileptic fits and delirium tremens and so on. Unless this crisis is radical enough, the person becomes so enamored of the almost womblike security of the death-in-life state that he re-forms the same pattern, collusively reinforced by certain others whom he gets to treat him essentialistically, as an object—"an alcoholic." The tracing out of the genesis in early life of this pattern of orality is clearly a matter of psychoanalytic work, but I shall parenthesize this area and concentrate on the nature of the relation of secondary (false) control to primary (true) control.

I suspect that most people do not even get near the choice between primary and secondary control as basic issues in their lives because they are simply controlled from the outside almost all the time. But I think we have to define the nature of true, primary control or discipline. Essentially, this seems to me to take the form of a promise—a promise that runs through every form of departure, every voyage of death and rebirth—the promise to stay wholly and holy in the world, in a redefined sense of the sacerdotal. Discipline, then, is a mode of staying in the world, in the sense of being actively engaged in the world through the thick and thin of ecstatic joy and the most far-reaching despair. The promise that defines discipline, however, must be made not only internally but also, at least implicitly, to others. The pain of the promise is immense: it is a terminal agony that one passes through to see one's life and the world from the other side of a certain death. In this sense it is more than self-containment and should not be mistaken for self-containment, as it may involve moments of spilling over the lip of the cup of the self. But the promise must in some form be registered on the world, with a simultaneously promised refusal of the possibility of retracting or breaking it.

More than this, discipline is a sort of antithermostat. Most people turn on and then turn off automatically, that is to say, in a fairly well expected, ritualistic way. The Man of Discipline turns on and off entirely by an option that is conditioned by his sense of the rightness and openness of the human context and his sense of the right moment in the interplay of his time system with those of others. Also, discipline should not be mistaken for the meta-level control of (false) control shown by people who have not entered the region of primary control—however impressive this control of control may seem to be.

Discipline thus is life-affirming, insofar as it conditions the possibility of good after-death experiences within life, experiences that renew the person rather than leave him lost in the limbo of the static deathlike state of the person who is caught up in systems of false control. Most people said to be mad or schizophrenic are in fact aiming at discipline in this sense, but betray themselves by collusive involvement with their families and psychiatric institutions because they know of no way by which they may find other people who know about the discipline they are trying to attain—and there certainly is an objective scarcity of such other people. I think that ultimately it will take nothing less than a mass social revolution and the overthrowing of bourgeois power structures to create these human possibilities.

But then, even in a revolutionary society like Cuba the family-psychiatric collusion tends to persist,[31] although the human conditions now exist for the abolition of psychiatric units in any forms. When in Cuba in 1968 I proposed a pilot scheme for one region over two years

31 Not only because of native circumstances but because of the importation of a bourgeoisified Soviet model of the family and psychiatry.

whereby anyone showing unusual behavior (for instance, taking his clothes off and sitting in the middle of the road) would be taken into the house of someone in the community and simply cared for by people who would sit with him, under the supervision of an elder of the local Committee for the Defense of the Revolution or the Women's Federation. If people could be dealt with thus without hospitalization, a nationwide extension of the plan would hopefully avoid any psychiatrization of people within five years. A remaining nucleus of United States-trained psychiatrists, however, seem to be imaginatively remote from such a model. One can only hope that the "New Man" one day soon will penetrate the psychiatric front, but there seems to me to be a good case for the avant-garde of first-world psychiatry (i.e., anti-psychiatry) entering onto this scene in a real (i.e., dehierarchizing) socialist country.

I have referred to these matters, since the conventional practice of clinical psychiatry is aimed at producing the peculiar stasis of death-in-life wherever an impulse to true discipline shows itself indiscreetly enough. In other words, psychiatry is a massive police operation that would extend itself without limit—hence the mushrooming of more and more out-patient clinics and "community care" facilities that simply objectify and categorize the victims and endlessly multiply prescription forms for pills to shut people up. A true, waking, noncategorized death and after-death experience simply requires the right people to be around one. Then one can look back on one's whole life—past, present and future—by an act of dying in it, seeing it with the eyes of death and then returning in the mode of a rebirth, of opening new eyes.

In the meantime, people all over the world are dying of starvation or, in guerrilla struggles, from the far more direct and obvious assault of imperialism. I have said before in this book that I shall concentrate on the situation in the first world and the modes of revolutionary activity possible in that context, but if one is to write about death and revolution an extension of range seems clearly necessary.

It is naive and psychologistic to speak of the death of the third world as an externalization of the undied death of the first world, so let us try to make this situation more phenomenologically true, that is, truer in direct experience. It is true, of course, that the first world is dying its own death by ecological autodestruction, rendering the environment unlivable by a blind technological Gadarene plunge. But this is not enough to account for the shift of locus of actual violent death. One gets a little closer to the truth if one considers how the first world actually *deprives itself* of death in this sense: death in first-world countries is conventionalized and ritualized to a remarkable degree. One has an assortment of statistically likely "causes of death" to "choose" from, and there is a certain class determination of these diseases. For instance, the self-employed *petit bourgeois* who has a coronary thrombosis will probably die very quickly of it, because he cannot face the consequences of loss of income and what seems to him to be intolerable poverty. The entrepreneur with large reserves of capital may be able to afford to take it easy and live through many years of occasional "heart trouble," as may (in Britain) a worker who has been conditioned to resign himself to the meager benefits of National Assistance and the facilities of the National Health Service.

So one dies one's elected death with the total anonymity of the category one selects or is elected into. Death is unpublic and covert—above all, it is unwitnessed and unmourned. In fact, it does not seem to happen at all. A middle-aged working-class woman told me that when her mother died (in November, in England) there had been a full-scale family meeting to decide the issue of burial and cremation. The most outspoken "leader"-member of this family finally decided the issue in these terms: "If she's buried, we're all likely to catch cold standing around that grave—she wouldn't want that. If she's cremated, at least we'll all be warm!" They got warm.

But the full significance of the death of a particular person to particular other persons was submerged in a defensive, unconscious joke.

When one comes onto the reactions to death in the middle classes, the horrors are far greater because they are so much more tortuously disguised. It's all very respectable. In one family I knew very well, the grandmother waited after her husband's death, until the age of ninety-four, for her three sons to die, one after the other; now, three years later, she is waiting for the death of her two grandsons, and after that she has one great-grandson to go. She may wait on awhile. In the meantime, the other family members wait on her, turn her after each successive stroke to avoid bedsores, wash her, feed her and complain endlessly about how difficult she is. Nobody will mourn her, and all of them will secretly pretend not to be glad that she's gone—just relieved for "her sake."

There are certain hospitals in this country that "incurable" people go to die in. Well, maybe that death clinic might be brought into relation with the "life clinic," if that is not too preposterous a term for the conventional obstetric unit. And maybe the death-life clinic should be open for anyone to come in and witness and help and be taught about death by the dying—as if the dying knew what they know.

In many French villages the cart or van that carries away the garbage is disguised, on occasions of death, as the local hearse. Or perhaps it's the other way round. At least there is an incipient honesty in this particular ambiguity.

All deaths in the first world are murder disguised as suicide disguised as the course of Nature.

In the third world all deaths, more simply, are murder. No disguise is necessary. How do we compassionately put to death the murderers or, better, put to death the murderousness of the murderers? Perhaps by showing them, with a requisite counterviolence, the nature of their own suicide. But that means an act of self-exposure in which the self that one exposes is a dead self, one's own death. One does not expose oneself to others, primarily because self-exposure means exposure of one's self to one's self. The man who rapes a child and then kills her or him is usually caught up in this disclosing of the reality of his death to himself that then becomes so terrifying to him that he has rapidly to evacuate it into the death of the child. The rape is perfunctory, and the death of the child is not murder but a traceable extension of the suddenly realized and immediately refused death of the quasi-rapist, quasi-murderer. Nothing corporeally real happens on this scene until the whole society (that's "us") demands the sacrificial offering of the mutilated body of a child victim.

How do we turn around the signs at the entrance of the psychiatric prison so that we can see ourselves as the violently disturbed inmates of a rather larger bin? "They" hurt or kill one or two other people, if that. "We" normal people murder not only them but countless millions of people across the world. The behavioral patterning of "them" and "us" is identical. The extent of destruction in "our" case, involving all the rationalizations of imperialism over the whole world scene, is incomparable with "theirs"—it is just so much bigger and so much less in the light of day.

The acid test as to whether this identity of patterning amounts to "psychologism," that is to say, the reduction of a complex social reality to the actual or inferred workings of the mind of a particular person, lies entirely in the domain of the actual experience of the observer. The experiential resonances of feeling for me identify the two levels of event without the need for recourse to mediating structures that lie in between and hence on neither of these two levels. The meditation resides precisely in the upsurge of inspecting-feeling in the engaged observer. Imperialism *is* the rapist-murderer (no longer appearing normal, as most rapist-murderers do), finally gone mad. Bourgeois society, to sustain itself, invents various categories of madness. The true direction of the diagnostic arrows that point to certain victims should be reversed to their source, which is the absent hearts and the absent-mindedness of each of us who support the structures of this society.

It would be absurd to pretend to be prescriptive in some unifying way when one realizes that the various schisms and partings between radical activist groups are not only inevitable but in fact also enriching to the cause of the first-world revolution. It is only when hierarchizing bureaucratization passes a certain limit, as is the case in most first-world communist parties, that concerted revolutionary activity becomes limited in its effect by collusive maneuvering with bourgeois power structures. Revolution in the only current, viable sense entails both an external, mass-social, and internal, personal and private, divorce from all the machinations of capitalist-imperializing society. It means more than, say, a reformist infiltration of mass media or a strategically planned but transparently ungenuine and disingenuous reformism in the region of student life. It means a clear enactment of our desires that may risk our lives if we cannot risk meeting our deaths.

The Situationist pamphlet "Theses on the Commune" refers to the Commune as the greatest carnival of the nineteenth century, but to try to burn down the Louvre is merely symbolic. Revolutionary activity has to move beyond the symbolic into the phase of literalization of the stasis of "working" institutions in bourgeois society. If these institutions are stripped objectively (because we can see them as subsisting in a manner that merely pretends growth), what we can now do is to stop the stopping of any realization that the people who would stop others have stopped their own realization of their passive violence that actively destroys the rest of the world, as well as obscures the first-world source of the violence.

All strategies become evasion in the sense of a false seeking for comforting solidarity. Solidarity can never be arrived at before its actual invention in work and struggle. That work and struggle are the autonomous emanations of individuals and small groups implies, not a fragmentation of revolutionary effort, but simply an affirmation of the purity of the effort in its only remaining historically actual form.

Most radical strategies sadly amount to introspective game-playing that eschews the rigor and rigors of the world outside the small group of ten to a hundred and ten people.

In the third world, strategies are necessary and the captain has to be the last one aboard the sinking ship. In the first world, the captain jumps into a lifeboat first because that is what he wants to do anyhow, and if he weighs enough it will keep the ship afloat marginally longer. But not, I hope, too long. The ship will sink and we will have to swim by our own chosen routes to the other shore. At the moment we are all embarked on the same ship, but on different voyages. In one sense, the more different the better, but how much difference can we personally contain? If we let the ship sink we may find our own way, or we may drown—which may be our own way—or we may find two square yards where we can rest on the shore before getting up to find our totally real and totally invisible sustenance.

The good feed we are after will certainly exceed orality and may in fact be a pebble held in one's cheek. That is a bit better than holding one's tongue in one's cheek when there is an urgent cry, beyond any personal utterance, for someone to tell the truth. The logical structure of "telling," in its total deployment in language, is ambiguous here. To tell, in the linguistic origins of this word, means anything in between counting numbers of entities of any sort and recounting, which is a poetic act of violence against arithmetic. Recounting means telling a true tale that inexorably pisses across the face of multiplication tables and compassionately enough makes a joke of the absurdity by which some people think they are teaching other people that two and two don't make five or six or three. To make four possible, we have to proscribe it as a possibility until we are ready to accept it or deny it. The Empedoclean plunge is simply where we are all falling—into our own Mount Etnas. The tragedy of the Gadarene slope resides in the spurious cure of the possessed man who dispossessed himself of his madness and put it into pigs. There is no miracle in the refusal of the arsehole of swine that so plaintively invites a just bestiality.

To tell the truth is by no means the obverse of telling a lie. There are lying truths and truthful lies. Capitalized truth (the Truth) is the vision of this ambiguity and its systematic, ironizing usage in the world, in a way that refuses both games on the small social scale and strategies on the larger social scale.

Truth accepts its funniness while refusing the comic and the spurious comfort of any sort of humor. At the same time, it is not humorless because the parameter humorousness/humorlessness is irrelevant to its operations in the world.

Truth is an unspeakable madness
Truth is a lethal awakening
Truth is the revolver of revolution.
Revolution has become equated with
the minute hand of a clock sweeping
around its face always reaching the same point
in a historical line.
Truth is the unimpeded vision of the face
that is its own Clear Light already
achieved as the end in the present that
can no longer be ahead of the present.
Truth is death made viable
Truth, with a deceptive advance into
simplicity, is what we are going
to do—
Now, which now and then is not then,
But probably now.

The moral of this tale is that death must no longer be accepted submissively but rather must be feared with increasing intensity. Certainly the fear must be contained, but death must begin to live from the very moment that we give birth to it. When we begin to enter into the labor pains, which is not quite the same thing as going into labor, we may find that a beautiful baby falls out of our laps, into our own accoucheur hands, a baby with the discernible countenance of our death.

I once knew a man who felt that lying down, much less sleeping, would mean his dying. His bed, if he lay down, would pulsate with his heartbeat, always just a little ahead of his own pulse. So he stayed up, quite correctly, until he dropped in a proper exhaustion. Any one of us can have a Berry aneurysm, a swelling on an artery in the brain that can be quite undiagnosable, that can burst at any moment and kill us within seconds. Before I finish writing this sentence and before you finish reading it, you or I might drop down dead. And of course, any of us may die any night in our sleep. All we know is that we will know about those modes of death in good time, time beyond the few recognized seconds. Being duly attentive, we know about our deaths now, and we know that all fully witnessed deaths are revolutionary deaths. By a compassionate integration of our deaths we befriend this part of our lives, but friendship means a maximizing terror that amounts to a bit more than love in terms of sheer commitment.

Friendship is a bit more difficult than love because the option of separateness that I have regarded as centrally definitive of love is in this case not optional but already selected.

"I went to a demonstration by myself with some friends." If enough people see that, Grosvenor Square will finally be on fire.

Death is the end of solidity elucidated through the discovery of a wholly nonsubstantial solidarity.

> I am not telling riddles because the riddle
> speaks my name and calls me to it.
> The riddle at least knows my right name
> and tells me what it is.

But I still cannot hear because the resonances of the appellation are too deep and too still for my ears—ears that are persistently stuck in an unending but paradoxically limited human acoustic range beyond which I've forgotten most sounds and certainly the most important sounds, unless they become a pleasantly intrusive noise. Noise is welcome by virtue of the ease of its refusal.

Death is the freedom to scream and to gurgle one's last breath away *within* life—but there are few places to do this safely enough. I think we have to create desert areas in the metropolis where people can scream without interference.

There is one consolation in all this: our deaths will wait for us if we can wait for them.

Silence and waiting are always difficult, but the waiting and the silence circumscribe the heart of revolution. If we wait a little longer, the silence may become that heart.

# My Last Will and Testament

THE TALMUD SAYS: "Before God made the world, he held a mirror to the creatures, that in it they might behold the sufferings of the spirit and the raptures that ensue therefrom. Some of them took up the burden of suffering. But others refused, and those God struck out of the Book of Life."

The unclear and ruthless God who, unjustifiably but with justice, is supposed to have said that is a totally false and totally arrogant creature, pushed out of the minds of people who refuse any recognition of their arrogance, in the interest of a socially demanded humiliation that screws, screws up and is screwed up by any dawning light of humility.

But let us take these words lexicologically, that is, far too simply. The last will is the last thing in the world that anyone wants to will or wants to will to will, since any will will be a mirroring of extraneousness that converts us from being persons into being impersonations of any person we might at any moment be. The last "will," very precisely, is the lost desire. So maybe we will not make wills any more, but rather will will to will to be willing to crowd our desires out of the undreamable region of fantasy and the nonactualizable lacuna of a refused desire, so that we will lose the lost last will and then write out a properly legal form that will look like a poem or a song or may be drawn, rather than drawn up, a will that will translate my will into taking what I want from the world before you read this—you other people.

The word "testament" plunges us into the visual. If it is done properly, it means seeing that one has never been seen. So that stranded in the vacuity of ordinary social intercourse (intercourse, that is, a sort of running between other people which is supposed to mean running off the tracks prescribed by the normal unwhole, unholy world that pretends itself as unhealable) we start to bear witness ourselves, for the first time in this peculiar testamentary deposition. We inspect our bodies, feel the hardening of our pricks, the fluctuating tensions of our cunts and, with a correctly positioned mirror, convert a fully testified-to turd into our birth that our last will and testament will deny unless we will that it won't.

How do we convert the conventional testament into some sort of gift, so that no longer will flowers be put on graves, but rather, they will grow like a good grass from the beautiful and beatific manure that will be the gently encouraging putrefaction of our properly died bodies? If we are to make a renewed testament that eludes the "perfect ends" of the Old and New Testaments, we have to know a bit more about the meaning of a gift. Testamentation here has to relinquish the carefulness of the witnessing act and ingest a huge pipeful of absurdity to become witless enough to stop witnessing and to give and to receive. But the ambiguity of the gift must be fully registered if we will not perpetuate the established forms of social violence that I have been writing about in this book.

Going back to Old Norse and Middle High German, on to present-day Dutch and German, we find that generally "gift," in the female gender, means a donation issuing from a feeling of generosity. In the neuter, "gift" means poison. What a gift means in the masculine gender has never been linguistically decided; perhaps historically it has been placed too remote from any range of social choice.

Men are men. One day they will become people, but we have to continue the witless witnessing of our testament to get the full feel of the body-and-mind cavity that men are out of.

Men in first-world countries persecute the third world, as well as minorities within the first world, including the major "minority" called women, on the clearly visible base of their envy of negritude, which is colorful, and of procreation, which is alive. There are thousands of spermatozoa in each ejaculation, but there is only one egg in the woman that is going to save one particular sperm from the usual fate of all sperms. Ejaculations are largely contingent and indifferent in this sense. Men are so cocksure, that perhaps orgasm is actually less common in men than in women.

Blackness, as I have said, in physical, scientific terms, is all colors in fantastic concentration. The white man has lost color because he is terrified of his envies. His blood has drained out of his facial tissue because of a perpetual and perpetuated unrecognized fear. The classical interpretation, in terms of the white man's fear of his potency, is more irrelevant than ludicrous. The white man envies the black man's *color* quite simply. Genocidal war against black men is the standard defense against this envy, and there is a clear relation, although not an equation, between race murder and the subjugation of women.

Revolution, I believe, will only become a total enough social reality when white men can assume all the colors of blackness and then have babies too.

In Cuba, the Guevarist doctrine of the New Man gets very close to the extended sense of revolution that I have pursued in these pages. The New Man is the pragmatic revolutionary who effectively annihilates the power structures of the feudal, bourgeois state and takes whatever power he needs to maintain an autonomous community, which he learns how to defend with guns, but at the same time he uses Marxist theory as a technique of being in the world in such a way that exploitative relations can never be reconstructed, and if bureaucratic hierarchization begins to emerge, it can be very quickly brought down. Bureaucratic tendencies persist, of course, in Cuba still, only eleven years after its liberation, but I found no evidence that people there would tolerate for long the imposition of sclerosed forms of nonlife on them.

The reason for this original revolutionary success in the Cuban case resides in other characteristics of the New Man that I shall try to delineate. Those of the original revolutionaries with a Spanish Catholic bourgeois past broke out from this past with a poetic, visionary leap that made possible a conjunction of revolutionary effort with supposedly superstitious poor peasants and above all with the spirit of voodoo in the Afro-American people—a spirit that, however hidden and implicit it remains, defines in experience the perpetual possibility of regeneration. So one finds, if one examines the ideology of the New Man, a curious syncretism that ranges from the shamanistic origins of voodoo to proto-Christianity (the idea of the New Man in Saint Paul, before Christianity became institutionalized and counterrevolutionary) and, then, the full integration of these lines of light from a remote past in the present illumination of a perpetually renewed Marxism that is in fact quite opposite to revisionism.

I think that we can now begin to define a link between third-world forms of revolution and what must be at the heart of revolutionary transformation in the first world. Once when I spoke at a mass meeting to celebrate the anniversary of the Cuban revolution, I asked the people there how many of them were prepared at this stage to die in the cause of socialist revolution. One nice young man told me afterwards that he thought he was. The question was both ironic and direct. I think that in a direct way we certainly have now to be able to risk our lives on the streets in urban guerrilla warfare—it took me thirty-six years to reach that point, but some of us are getting there much quicker. But to penetrate further into the full ambiguity of "risking one's life," I think we have to see this as a courageous movement out of any form of social stasis in which we may have got ourselves comfortably enmeshed. I mean, for instance, existence within settled, monogamous forms of family life that limits one's work and love relationships and creates a destructive impingement on the lives of everyone who comes into contact with us. I have discussed this before as the "illusion of the quantifiability of love."

Also, one has to find the courage to move, at any required moment, out of institutional work situations that would destroy us with their false familylike security, and then find other ways of surviving cooperatively in the prerevolutionary West. In fact, what I am getting at now is that, given a certain illuminating despair, "risking one's life" becomes synonymous with risking one's life to save one's life. There is no generosity in the conventional suicides that we elect for ourselves in terms of family and work. There is also certainly no self-love in that and therefore no possibility of a truly unambiguous gift to others.

Philippe Ariès,[32] in a study of the social meaning of wills, has shown how the family before the mid-eighteenth century came into the life of the individual on occasions of crisis within life or after death. Only since the mid-eighteenth century has the family invaded the day-to-day life of its members to a point where the quotidian existence of persons becomes almost totally family-occupied territory—the territory, factually, of most violent crime, including murder (often disguised as "battered babies"), in our society. All murders are family murders, either within a literal family or in family-replica situations.

The family form of social existence that characterizes all our institutions essentially destroys autonomous initiative by its defining nonrecognition of what I have called the proper dialectic of solitude and being with other people. The family, over the last two centuries, has mediated an invasiveness into the lives of individuals that is essential to the continued operating of imperializing capitalism. The family, definitionally, can never leave one alone, as it is the hypostasization of the ultimately perfected mass medium. The family is the television box replete with color, touch, taste and smell effects that has been taught to forget how to turn off. No psychedelic drug will ever turn one on unless one can begin to turn off the right knobs on this family box. To turn off must be in terms of an evacuation or at least partial neutralization of the family presences and *family modes of functioning* (even more important than internalized family "objects") that exist in our heads, in terms of the family as a system that we superimpose all the time on everyone else, with an unknowing violence

32 "Wills, Tombs and Families," *New Society*, No. 356, September 25, 1969, pp. 473–75.

that invites their unknowing violation of the source of the unknowing violence—which is where we came in.

The time to write our last will and testament is now, and only one clause is essential and urgent. Nothing is to be left to the Family. Mothers, fathers, brothers, sisters, sons and daughters, husbands and wives have all predeceased us. They are not there as people to be left with anything of oneself or left anywhere in oneself. The blood of consanguinity has already flowed through the gutters of suburban family streets.

The age of relatives is over because the relative invades the absolute center of ourselves as we do his unless we get this will right.

Let us hope that at the end of our lives we are left with an immense if battered love to leave and also a finally defeated despair. And then let us leave these to men, to women, and to children.

I shall.

# Gnomic Gifts

THERE ARE probably six or eight ways of castrating a man, but the first two ways, which don't resort to the carving knife, are probably most important. You can either take the prick away from the man, or you can remove the man from his penis.

(From Ann)

Tiz, a psychologist, told me about a boy in a psychiatric prison who had cut off his mother's head and roasted it in the oven. My reflections on this story were that perhaps he was hungry.

Billie, aged eight, after a visit to his grandparents in New York, told me, "They're torturing me with food."

## HAPPY PREBIRTHDAY TO YOU

Why don't we add a year onto our lives on the anniversary of our births and celebrate the state of affairs going on one year before the day of our birth? At that stage there were two groups of chemical substances, one in each of our parents' bodies—a forming ovum in one of our mother's ovaries and an unformed sperm in one of our father's testicles. If, then, we can feel this chemical split profoundly enough, we may or we may not, of course, look forward to the impending chemical marriage because we can be sure that this is the only sort of marriage as a sheer event in the world—an event that shows the frightened social compulsivity of "marriage," in the ordinarily accepted sense, in its true light.

There certainly has to be a decision made about the limits of what is understandable about the social behavior of people achieved through "psychoanalysis" and "analytic psychotherapy." The intelligibility of human conduct may be carried further by the "existential" consideration of the possibility of the transcendence of all microsocial conditioning by certain critical acts of choice that carry one into new areas of conditioning that, again, can be refused by radical choice.

Beyond this we are plunged into regions of mystery that have to be apprehended, that is, knowingly grasped at and at least temporally held, because they cannot be seen in the peculiar light of the obscurity of a certain sort of vision that runs a gauntlet through the expertly arranged swords of mystification that consists in the multiplicity of defensively self-blinding games that go on between people who, in various ways, are personally and directly engaged with each other. Mystification is a mutually elected and engendered mode of nonseeing that defines itself as a social plan, that is a coordinated pile (refusing synthesis) of strategies and tactics, that is aimed at a destruction of vision, by which I mean the conjunction of light and obscurity in a given social whole. This designated social whole may be the beggars of Calcutta, who really live and are not well in the white ghettoes of New York and Chicago and the communes of San Francisco and Notting Hill Gate, or it may be the genocidally violated people of Southeast Asia and South Africa and Angola who, as we well know, live comfortably and well and are still convincedly voting their cadaveric assassins into a globally destructive semblance of power in the best parts of Greenwich Village, Neuilly-sur-Seine and Welwyn Garden City. Or it may be any family or friendship or network of people that you either know personally or might conceive of.

This arrival in the world, through any person, of demystified mystery is revolutionary in the moment that proceeds its institutional deformation into oscillating systems of suicide⟵⟶murder.

There once was a young man who, throughout his childhood until the age of nine, had longed for his father to chastise him. One day, at long last, his father actually raised his hand with the intention of hitting his son's backside. As he did this, the father landed a backsider on the face of his voyeuristic wife.

Heidi, aged four, after I had taught her the language of trees, how to shake hands with them the right way, and then to hear their differential responses, how to hear the tree say hello and how to overcome the silent withdrawal of certain other trees: "I think you're just nuts!"